New Windows on London's Past

Information Technology and the Transformation of Metropolitan History

New Windows on London's Past: Information Technology and the Transformation of Metropolitan History

edited by
Matthew Woollard

Association for History and Computing (UK)
Glasgow
2000

Published by:
Association for History and Computing (UK)
The Subject Centre
1 University Gardens
University of Glasgow
Glasgow
G12 8QQ

ISBN: 0 9539766 0 2

Printed by in Great Britain by University of Essex Printing Services

Contents

Preface
Derek Keene

Big cities—with their thronging populations, their endlessly replicated houses and households, their commerce and markets, and their elaborate systems of taxation and control—foster a culture of numbers and listing. This has been apparent in the ancient world, in the cities of medieval Italy, and of course in London. For millennia, enumeration and record have been perceived as essential tools for governing and securing complex societies, above all in the metropolis. Totals of people (alive or dead), buildings, and of things consumed have likewise been central to the boosterish rhetoric of city description, and underpin many modern historians' and sociologists' attempts to explore and explain urban life. Sciences of society reflect the established dynamic of the society itself. For urban historians the new tools of information science and the computer fit into a recognisable intellectual tradition, but at the same time enormously enlarge the boundaries of what it is possible to explore. Had the computer been available to the thirteenth-century friar Bonvesino della Riva, he would undoubtedly have used it to elaborate and magnify his classic text on 'The Big Things of Milan'.

The essays and analyses in this collection, ranging over some four centuries, mirror Bonvesino's response to the numbers he found in the records and collective memories of his native city. Of course, historians increasingly make use of computers in their studies of very different sets of information, such as images, artefacts, and texts which do not have the standardised formats and content of the sources employed here. Nevertheless, the quantitative approach which characterises these essays is likely to retain a key role in metropolitan history, not least because it replaces estimation by certainty (or awareness of uncertainty) and so while answering some questions provides firm bases from which to pose new ones. The interaction between source and technique is central to each of the papers. Jim Galloway's paper uses the more or less standardised records of debt cases in one of the central law courts to provide for the first time robust measures of London's role as a source of credit and a focus of distributive trade in late medieval England, distinguishing the interests of different mercantile groups. Craig Spence explains the principles underlying the construction of a substantial database incorporating the first really comprehensive and systematic taxation records for early modern London, generated in response to state's pressing need for money during the 1690s. He also illustrates some of the ways in which the information can be used to reveal the social and economic geography of the metropolis. Both of these studies have had to confront problems of comparability arising from sources which do not consistently meet the historian's hopes or expectations. Graham Mooney shows how a similar problem was overcome in the context of an investigation of the changing causes of death in Victorian London. Computer technology and archival research made equally essential contributions to the process of adjusting the Registrar General's totals of deaths so as to allow for those who died at hospitals or other institutions but had lived outside the district where the institution lay. The outcome is a radical revision of the crude mortality rate for some key London districts. In a longitudinal analysis of census returns for Bethnal Green between 1891 and 1921 Kevin Schürer reveals important characteristics of immigrants and the labour market, not least the way in which Jewish families adapted traditional structures and practices to a new and harshly competitive environment.

All four essays demonstrate the striking historical insights which can be obtained, and the substantial resources created, by the use of simple and inexpensive computing techniques. The first three also show the value of computer mapping, both by points and by areas, for revealing the character and impact of the metropolis. Strikingly, the way in which the data for Bethnal Green were anonymised for use by the historian involved the annihilation of spatial relationships within the neighbourhood, thus making it impossible, as yet, to answer several questions arising from Schürer's paper. The first three papers arise from projects at the Centre for Metropolitan and are based on presentations made at a study day on computing and metropolitan history held at the

Centre in June 1998, at which Edmund Green also gave a presentation on the Westminster Historical Database project based at Royal Holloway, University of London. The fourth arises from research based at the Cambridge Group for the History of Population and Social Structure and the University of Essex.

This sort of historical computing is of special value for its fundamental contribution to knowledge, for the clarity of its results, and for the resources created which enable future study of related issues. One looks forward to more projects of this type and to arrangements which will encourage and facilitate the wider use of the data.

Centre for Metropolitan History, Institute of Historical Research

Reconstructing London's distributive trade in the later middle ages: the role of computer-assisted mapping and analysis

James A. Galloway

Medieval London played a central role in the networks of trade which distributed imported and manufactured goods across England, and which channelled native products and manufactures towards overseas markets.[1] A major centre of commerce and craft production since Roman times, London's status as an economic centre of gravity became increasingly important as its political and cultural leadership were enhanced during the period c.1000–1300.[2] The great size of the pre-Black Death city enabled it to mould productive and distributive systems across an extensive area, and to promote economic specialisation in the small towns of its hinterland. Reduced in size after the famines and plagues of the early and mid-fourteenth century, London continued to increase its relative dominance of England's urban system, accumulating a growing share of the nation's taxable wealth. Foreign trade was also drawn to the capital, which handled nearly a third of the recorded total at the beginning and end of the fourteenth century, and over two-thirds by the end of the fifteenth. This rapid leap forward is the more remarkable in that it occurred during a century characterised by stagnant population and an adverse economic climate. London's greater resources and superior access to international trade and credit networks seem to have enabled it to weather recession–particularly severe during the period from c.1440–1470–more successfully than its provincial rivals, whose overseas commerce and merchants were increasingly drawn to the capital.[3]

The growing dominance of London within English overseas trade seems to have been paralleled by an increased share in internal commerce, although the absence of a statistically-based source comparable to the customs accounts makes its study more difficult. There are obvious reasons for believing that the two things would go together, however, as the accumulation of produce for export and the distribution of imported goods would of necessity be increasingly centred upon the port which handled such a large proportion of total trade. Although much has been written on the activities of the London companies whose members participated in distributive trades, to date no attempt has been made systematically to measure the extent of the capital's predominance within this field of commerce, or to identify the extent of the economic hinterland which it supplied with high-valued imports and manufactures. The most recent and detailed study of the grocers, one of the city's principal mercantile companies, has relatively little to say about spatial aspects of their distributive trade.[4] An earlier study concluded that London's grocers and mercers had customers 'from all parts of the country', although the connections cited from a range of sources in fact pointed to a predominant interest in the midlands and the south.[5] The issue is an important one, both for a fuller understanding of the commerce that sustained the capital during the later middle ages and for a wider appreciation of processes at work in the economy of England at that period. The increasing predominance of London has been linked to the 'crisis' experienced by many provincial towns in the fifteenth and early sixteenth centuries. Furthermore, to understand fully the rapid expansion of London in the later sixteenth and seventeenth centuries and its full emergence as an 'engine of economic growth' within the English economy it is necessary to explore the degree to which its economic centrality had become established during the later middle ages. The spatial extension of the capital's economic hinterland at this time may have played a crucial role in the development of integrated markets and the regularisation of inter-regional trade.

This article illustrates the way in which the computer-assisted mapping and analysis of a copious and previously under-exploited documentary source is adding to our knowledge of the structure and spatial extent of London's distributive trade around the year 1400, at or close to the beginning of the period of the most rapid increase in the city's dominance of overseas trade. It describes the principal sources and methods used, and presents some initial findings regarding the extent and structure of London's economic hinterland c.1400, and the varied forms of distribution employed by some of the city's most important mercantile groupings at that date.

The mapping of regional or national data-sets compiled from documentary sources was a central part of the practice of medieval historical geography which developed in Britain during the first half of the twentieth century, associated particularly with scholars such as H. C. Darby and R. A. Pelham; in their hands mapping became a powerful tool to illustrate themes such as the distribution of population and wealth at the time of Domesday and the organisation of the textile industry in later medieval England. Such approaches became increasingly unfashionable during the 1960s and 1970s, as human geography as a whole sought to align itself more firmly with the main-stream social sciences, many practitioners seeking to adopt 'critical' or 'humanistic' positions and implicitly or explicitly rejecting what was sometimes caricatured as the 'crude empiricism' of drawing dots on maps.[6] The 1980s and 1990s have, however, seen a notable revival of interest in the spatial organisation of the medieval economy, although much of the work has been undertaken outside geography departments. Studies of animate and non-animate power sources in the medieval countryside, of agrarian productivity and specialisation, and of the spatial organisation of the market economy have all effectively incorporated mapping into their methodology, and have played an important part in the re-conceptualisation of medieval England as a much more commercialised, urbanised and dynamic economy than had previously been believed.[7] At the heart of that economy was London, a city already capable of organising space and promoting specialisation in both production and distribution.[8]

Sources and methodology

The main source drawn upon in this reconstruction of London's role in the internal and distributive trade of later medieval England is the plea rolls of the Court of Common Pleas, one of the principal royal courts of England during the medieval and early modern periods. The court, which normally sat at Westminster, heard personal actions of various sorts, but by the second half of the fourteenth century was dominated by pleas of debt, brought by plaintiffs from throughout England. Attorneys were widely used, making the court accessible even to those living at a great distance from Westminster. The Court of Common Pleas was extensively used by London citizens at this period for the recovery of sums of money owed to them by defendants whose residence and occupation is frequently and, after 1413, almost universally stated. The affiliation of Londoners appearing as plaintiffs or defendants is normally recorded, thus making it possible to reconstruct distinctive patterns of contact pertaining to individual city companies as well to the capital as a whole. Although details of these debts are only infrequently recorded, the combination of occupational and residential data often allows the content of debt relations to be inferred.

Cases were initiated by writ, and their progress is recorded in the termly plea rolls, which constitute one of the most voluminous document classes in the Public Record Office.[9] In the decades around 1400 each of the four term rolls for every year contain some 500–600 membranes, each of which may record details of up to twenty causes currently in progress before the court. After an apparent dip in the volume of litigation in the late-fifteenth and early-sixteenth centuries the bulk of the rolls increases rapidly after c.1550–by the later sixteenth century each term's rolls might contain up to 3,000 membranes.[10] This mass of documentation is not only 'a monumental testimonial to the litigiousness of the English people, but, perhaps more importantly, is a reflection of the pervasive role of debt and credit in economic life.[11] Credit was advanced routinely to purchasers, in the form of deferred payment for goods supplied, or payment by instalments. Cash was loaned for various periods, although the interest charged is usually disguised by a variety of devices. In addition to commercial transactions and loans where one party had defaulted on an agreement, the Common Pleas cases probably contain a proportion of *de facto* registrations of agreements, where the court was being used to record a contract which is disguised as a dispute. Where the details of cases are stated, the majority can be seen to relate to commercial transactions concerning the sale of goods, ranging from high-value textiles down to ironwork or agrarian produce. This mass of debt litigation can be taken as a good reflection of at least a part of the internal trade of England–a minimum value of 40s. applied to cases heard by the court, and so the petty debts for small sums or low-value goods which dominate the proceedings of most manorial and borough courts are excluded.

The great bulk of the Common Plea records, which exist in almost uninterrupted sequence from the later thirteenth century onwards, necessitates sampling. In the course of the research project 'Market networks in the London region: the trade in agrarian produce c.1400' a database of some 7,800 debts was constructed from three sampled Common Plea rolls, those for Michaelmas term 1384, 1403 and 1424.[12] The selection of these particular rolls was made with the aim of providing a representative coverage of the period c.1375–1425, taking into account the condition and completeness of the rolls, and the need to avoid years of particularly high prices, or of economic crises which might distort the pattern of debt litigation. Details of all debt pleas which were 'laid', that is, where the cause of the action was said to have originated in, London or ten surrounding counties were collected from these three rolls, and entered into a relational database.[13] A lengthy process of editing was then required to eliminate duplicate entries, identify and modernise place-names, add Ordnance Survey grid references, standardise occupational and status designations, and convert monetary values into a standard format. The resulting database permits extensive statistical analysis and mapping, to reveal characteristic patterns of economic activity and linkages.[14]

The overview that can be gained from analysis of the data is, however, wider than the geographical region indicated above, and can provide an insight into the interaction between London and the country as a whole. Examination of the Common Plea rolls from this period shows that Londoners rarely appeared as plaintiffs in cases laid outside London and immediately adjacent counties-that is to say, by collecting all cases attributed to London and the ten study–area counties we can be confident of having collected over 90 per cent and perhaps nearer to 99 per cent of all those with London plaintiffs which occurred in that term.[15] Work carried out subsequent to the creation of the main database, on the more distant counties of Devon, Staffordshire and Yorkshire, has confirmed that it was extremely rare for Londoners to lay pleas in those counties.[16] Londoners did indeed bring cases against residents of those counties, but when they did the actions were laid in London. The data thus provides us with a firm basis for reconstructing the overall pattern of contacts of Londoners, and in particular of those Londoners active within the distributive trades.

Elimination of duplicate entries caused by the return of particular actions to the court during the course of one law term resulted in a database containing 7,806 debt cases laid within the study area defined above. The numbers from the individual term rolls and the proportion of

London cases is shown in Table 1. Two striking facts emerge from the table. Firstly, there are significantly more debt pleas in the sample from 1403 than from 1384, and a further substantial increase between 1403 and 1424. Secondly, the number of debts laid in London increases at an almost identical rate, so that the proportion within the sample remains constant at 37–38 per cent. Although evidence from only three term rolls cannot be taken to establish a general trend, these data do not sit easily with those studies based on other debt-related sources that have indicated a substantial fall in activity during the late-fourteenth and early-fifteenth centuries. Studies by Nightingale and Kermode, based upon the analysis of Statute Merchant and Statute Staple certificates, indicate a sharp fall in certificates of debt and recognizances after the 1380s, both in London and the country at large, which is taken to indicate a corresponding contraction in credit within the economy.[17] The evidence presented here suggests that caution is needed in using the Statute certificates alone as indices of overall levels of credit or economic activity, as it appears that an increasing volume of debt litigation by Londoners and others was finding its way into Common Pleas at this period. Moreover, as we shall see, there is little doubt that a high proportion of these debts were of a mercantile nature.

Year	Number of debts	Number of debts Laid in London	London as a percentage of study area debts
1384	2089	798	38
1403	2605	978	38
1424	3112	1160	37
All years	7806	2937	38

Table 1. Numbers of debts collected from Michaelmas term rolls for study area (ten counties plus London)
Source: Common Pleas database.
Note: The figures represent the total number of cases extracted from the rolls, after elimination of duplicates caused by the return of an action to the court during a single term. They are a broadly accurate reflection of the total volume of Common Plea litigation within the London region but not a precise count, as each roll contains a few damaged membranes or illegible entries.

London's economic hinterland

The area that fed and fuelled medieval London, although very extensive compared to other English towns, was still largely confined to a group of surrounding counties. The principal exceptions to this generalisation were the regular coal supply from Tyneside, the crisis years supply of grain from the ports of Norfolk, Lincolnshire and occasionally further north, and the livestock trade, which was already reaching into the west midlands and perhaps beyond.[18] What of the wider economic hinterland with which London interacted—the area to which it supplied imported goods and extended credit and from which it obtained manufactures and primary products for export as well as for consumption? Was this hinterland 'regional' or 'national' in its scope—did London serve principally the south-east, or the whole of England? The Common Pleas database has permitted an attempt to answer that question and, for the first time, to produce a soundly-based map of medieval London's economic sphere of influence. This exercise rests upon analysis of 1,409 debts in the sampled material where the plaintiff was a Londoner and the residence of the defending party is specified.

In Figure 1 the relative density of debt contacts between London plaintiffs and non-London defendants is plotted at a county level, adjusted for county population at the time of the 1377 poll-tax.[19] This indicates an area of dense and moderately dense contacts extending west-east from Herefordshire to Suffolk, and south-north from Sussex to Rutland, with the greatest concentration of debtor residences in Middlesex, Surrey, Hertfordshire, Essex, Kent and Berkshire. Contacts between London and northern and south-western England were much less numerous. The mean distance between a London plaintiff and the residence of the debtor or alleged debtor from whom he sought to recover money was 114km (71 miles), and one-half of all the residences in the sample lay less than 88km (55 miles) from the city. The 'distance-decay' pattern is imperfect, however, with very low levels of interaction evident between the capital and the 'middle-distance' counties of Derbyshire and Shropshire, while in the far north London's contacts with Newcastle-on-Tyne raise Northumberland above the very low interaction levels found in the cases of Durham and Cumberland. Although debtors pursued by London plaintiffs lived in every county of England, the character of interaction was clearly much more attenuated in the area to

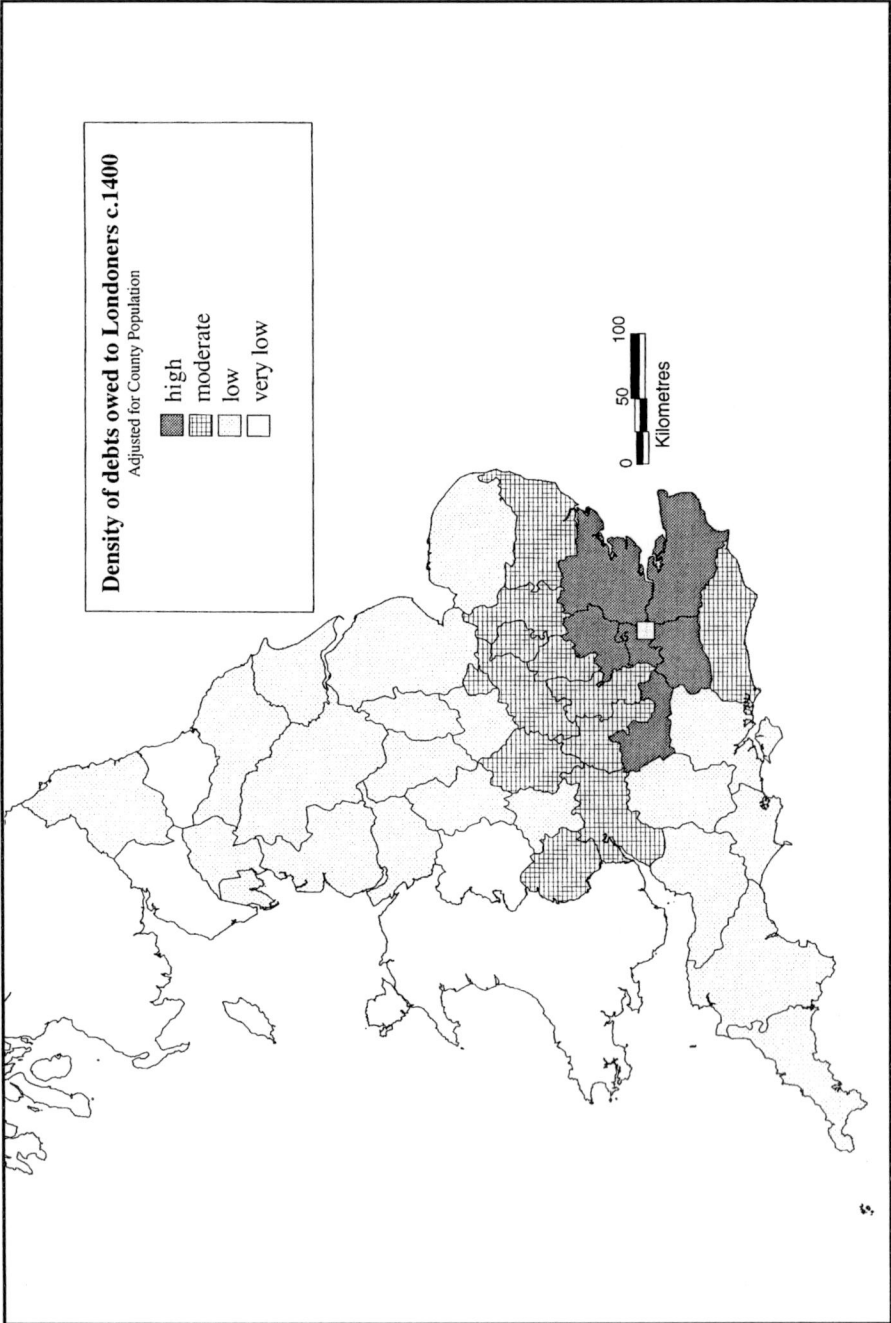

Density of debts owed to Londoners c.1400
Adjusted for County Population

- high
- moderate
- low
- very low

0 50 100
Kilometres

Figure 1. London's economic hinterland c.1400

the north-west of the Humber-Severn line and in the south-west. Overall, although London's economic hinterland was plainly very extensive, dwarfing those of even the largest of England's provincial towns, only in the loosest of senses could it be considered to have embraced all England by c.1400.[20]

The organisation of distributive trade

London's hinterland has thus far been considered in a highly generalised sense. Clearly, Londoners did not comprise a homogenous group, and the trade interests and hinterlands of different mercantile groupings were far from identical. Some of these differences can be reconstructed from the Common Pleas data. Although some individuals are simply described as 'of London', many are described as citizens and given an occupation or company affiliation.[21] In all, there are 96 different designations of this type in the sample, in addition to 23 status and clerical designations. The most frequently encountered affiliations are shown in Table 2.

Company affiliation	Number of debts in sample	Rank by number of debts	Position in Brewers' list, 1422
Mercer	425	1	1
Draper	342	2	3
Grocer	203	3	2
Skinner	166	4	7
Tailor	107	5	8
Fishmonger	83	6	4
Vintner	64	7	6
Stockfishmonger	52	8	-
Saddler	48	9	9
Goldsmith	47	10	5

Table 2. Most frequent company affiliation of London plaintiffs appearing in Common Pleas debt litigation c.1400

Source: Common Pleas database; Unwin, Gilds and companies, 370–1, (Brewers' list). See note 22.

The dominance of the big distributive groupings is immediately apparent; debts owed to mercers and drapers being particularly numerous. The rank-order by frequency of occurrence in the database is quite similar to the order in which 'all the crafts exercised in London' were listed in an entry in the Brewers' Company records compiled in 1422, which presumably reflected contemporary perceptions of the relative importance of the companies, at least as regards the wealthiest and most prominent of them.[22] There is a close agreement between these two rankings-one quantitative and the other essentially qualitative-in the composition of the top ten affiliations, the sole exception being the stockfishmongers who do not appear at all in the Brewers' list.[23] This correspondence adds to the plausibility of the Common Pleas debt evidence as providing an accurate reflection of economic activity and of the relative strength of the different groupings active within the capital's distributive trade. As is well known, the trading interests of members of London companies were diverse, citizens being permitted to trade wholesale in any kind of merchandise, but in most cases they still centred upon the 'core activities' indicated by the company names.[24] Thus, the core of the mercers' business was in luxury fabrics, the grocers' in imported spices and dyestuffs, and the vintners' in wine, although others also participated in those trades, and the members of these companies might deal in diverse other types of good. Members of virtually any company might have traded in woollen cloth, but the prominence of the mercers and the drapers in the records of debt litigation is undoubtedly a reflection of the central place that the trade in textiles occupied in the economic life of later medieval England.

	Mercer Plaintiff	Draper Plaintiff	Grocer Plaintiff	Skinner Plaintiff
1	Chapman (103)	Esquire (61)	Dyer (30)	Knight (32)
2	Knight (37)	Knight (48)	Chapman (18)	Esquire (28)
3	Esquire (28)	Gentleman (26)	Spicer (11)	Gentleman (16)
4	Gentleman (18)	Clerk (16)	Gentleman (8)	Skinner (15)
5=	Yeoman (7)	Draper (10)	Esquire (7)	Husbandman (4)
5=	Husbandman (7)	Parson (10)	-	-

Table 3. Most Common Occupation or Status of Debtors to London Mercer, Draper, Grocer and Skinner Plaintiffs c.1400
Source: Common Pleas database.
Note: No. of occurrences of each combination in brackets.

Members of all the principal London companies might deal directly with wealthy aristocratic or gentle consumers, even if they lived in quite remote parts of the country. This is well-illustrated by a collection of surviving bills issued by London merchants in the 1380s for goods supplied to Sir John Dinham, whose principal residences lay in south Devon. The drapers William Kyng and Thomas Frankeleyn and the mercer Richard Guy supplied diverse types of cloth to Dinham, as did John Bourwill, a tailor, who in addition charged for making gowns; Richard Loxleie, a grocer, supplied spices and imported foodstuffs such as rice and raisins; and the skinner John Tytesbyry sold Dinham costly furs.[25] It seems that Dinham did much of his London shopping in person, with payments made at a later date by his steward or receiver, a characteristic pattern for upper-class consumers of his period.[26] There were, however, important variations between the companies in the overall conduct of their domestic trade, and in particular, in the degree to which they made use of provincial merchants as middlemen. Some of these contrasts are illustrated in Table 3, where the most common occupation and status descriptions of debtors owing money to London mercer, draper, grocer and skinner plaintiffs are listed. The mercers conducted a substantial proportion of their trade with chapmen, small and middling provincial merchants who characteristically travelled to London to collect consignments of cloth and other goods, which they then retailed in their home town or region. By contrast, the drapers seem in the main to have dealt directly with aristocratic and gentle consumers, without the intervention of middlemen. A more diverse pattern is displayed in the debts claimed by grocers, many of which were owed by dyers, many resident in important cloth-making towns such as Salisbury and who had no doubt been supplied with imported woad and other dye-stuffs. Significant numbers of debts were also owed to grocers by chapmen, provincial spicers and gentle consumers. The skinners, like the drapers, were owed money first and foremost by aristocratic and gentle consumers, but a significant number of their debtors were provincial skinners whom they had doubtless supplied with imported furs wholesale.

The great majority of the appearances by Londoners in the Court of Common Pleas were as plaintiffs in debt actions, either in person or through an attorney, reflecting the active role of the capital's merchants in supplying goods and credit to merchants and consumers from elsewhere. Only 14 per cent of the Londoners' appearances in court were in the role of defendant, and of these nearly three-quarters involved plaintiffs who were themselves inhabitants of London or the suburbs of

Southwark and Westminster, reflecting intra-metropolitan trade and credit networks.[27] Table 4 summarises the data for London plaintiffs as a whole, and for members of the ten most frequently occurring affiliations.[28] The mean and median distance between London and the defendant's residence is shown, illustrating some clear contrasts in the extent of trading hinterlands. On average, of the ten most frequently-encountered groups, goldsmiths and vintners emerge as having the most spatially restricted hinterlands, mercers and skinners the most extensive.

Occupation/ affiliation of creditors	Debts specifying defendant residence	Debts with non-London defendant	Mean Distance of Debtors' residence from London	Mean Distance of Debtors' residence from London
	N.	N.	(km)*	(km)*
Mercers	281	270	138	109
Drapers	172	155	121	100
Grocers	175	168	111	98
Skinners	92	81	142	139
Tailors	50	43	108	81
Fishmongers	64	57	97	79
Vintners	35	31	73	51
Goldsmiths	26	18	66	51
Stockfishmongers	36	34	86	76
Saddlers	21	19	113	59
All London plaintiffs	1409	1283	114	88

Table 4. Extent and Structure of London's Distributive Hinterland c.1400
Source: Common Pleas database.
Note: Mean distance of debtors residence excludes London defendants.

The geography of distributive trade

Contrasts in the core commodities traded and in characteristic ways of doing business are quite closely reflected in the geography of the different companies' credit networks. The mercers, with their emphasis on wholesale trade and upon dealings with provincial chapmen, had geographically extensive contacts (Figure 2), dense in the counties around London, but extending strongly into the south-west and the eastern and north-eastern counties. The chapmen supplied the mercers with woollen cloth from the producing regions, and in turn distributed the Londoners' linens and other imports.[29] The mercers also directly supplied some specialist provincial merchants and retailers, such as the

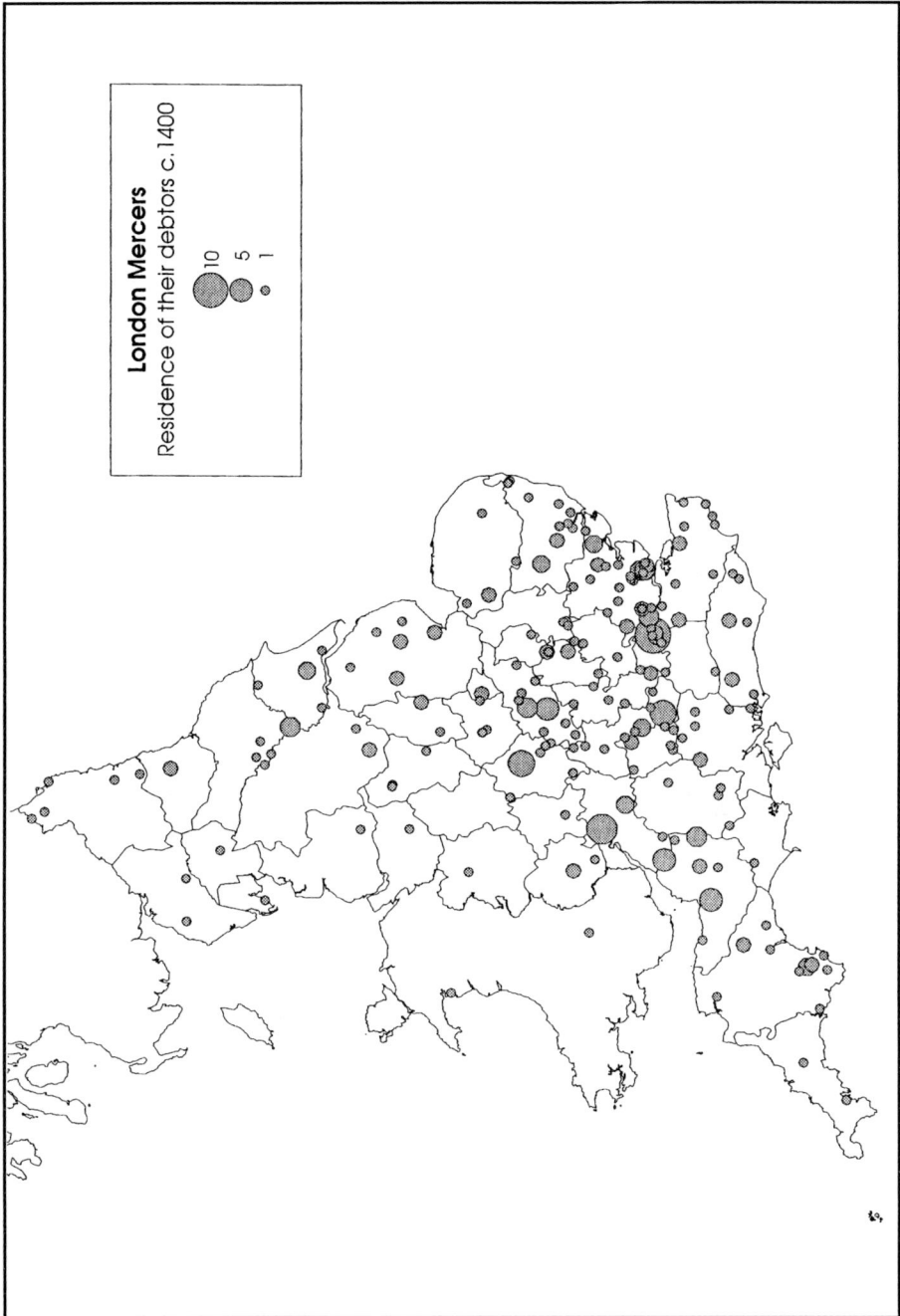

London Mercers
Residence of their debtors c.1400

10
5
1

Figure 2. Mercers' debtors c.1400

draper from Wick by Pershore in Worcestershire and the linen-draper from Havering in Essex who occur in the sample of debtors. Woolmen from Maldon and Colchester in Essex and Newark in Nottinghamshire also feature among the mercers' debtors, perhaps for non-delivery of wool for which advanced payment had been made, or for goods supplied to them for sale or personal consumption. A strong focus upon England's larger urban centres is also evident from the map, with Bristol, Gloucester, Bridgwater, Reading, Northampton and Coventry prominent among them.

The drapers' hinterland was somewhat more restricted (Figure 3), perhaps reflecting physical constraints upon direct dealing and retailing. The drapers' clients among the aristocracy and gentry must in the majority of cases have made their purchases in London, either in person or more frequently through a servant or agent, and transport costs would have discouraged such journeys from northern England.[30] The concentration of magnate residences in the capital provided additional opportunities for direct inspection of cloth and other goods before purchase, and led to the establishment of regular dealings between the aristocracy and individual London shopkeepers and merchants.[31] As with all the groupings, a significant minority of the drapers' debtors were fellow Londoners, including members of livery companies, churchmen and 'gentlemen'. Some distinctive strings of country residences are evident among the drapers' debtors, seemingly reflecting the road network, and are particularly prominent in the immediate vicinity of London, and in northern Essex and southern Suffolk. A different range of towns emerge as centres of contact, including York, which stands out as the only principal focus in the north, Salisbury, Norwich, Ely and Maidstone. Significantly, several of the debtors at York and Hull were described as merchants, suggesting that at this distance wholesale trade was as important to the drapers as retailing. This may also be true of contacts with Norwich, where the majority of the debtors were themselves described as drapers.

The grocers' trade hinterland was, again, more restricted than that of the mercers (Figure 4), with a strong concentration of debtor residences in Essex and such major cloth-making towns and regional centres as Coventry, York and, above-all, Salisbury, reflecting the supply of dye-stuffs to provincial industry. Some cloth-exporting grocers are known to have exchanged dyes directly for cloth, thus avoiding the need for cash

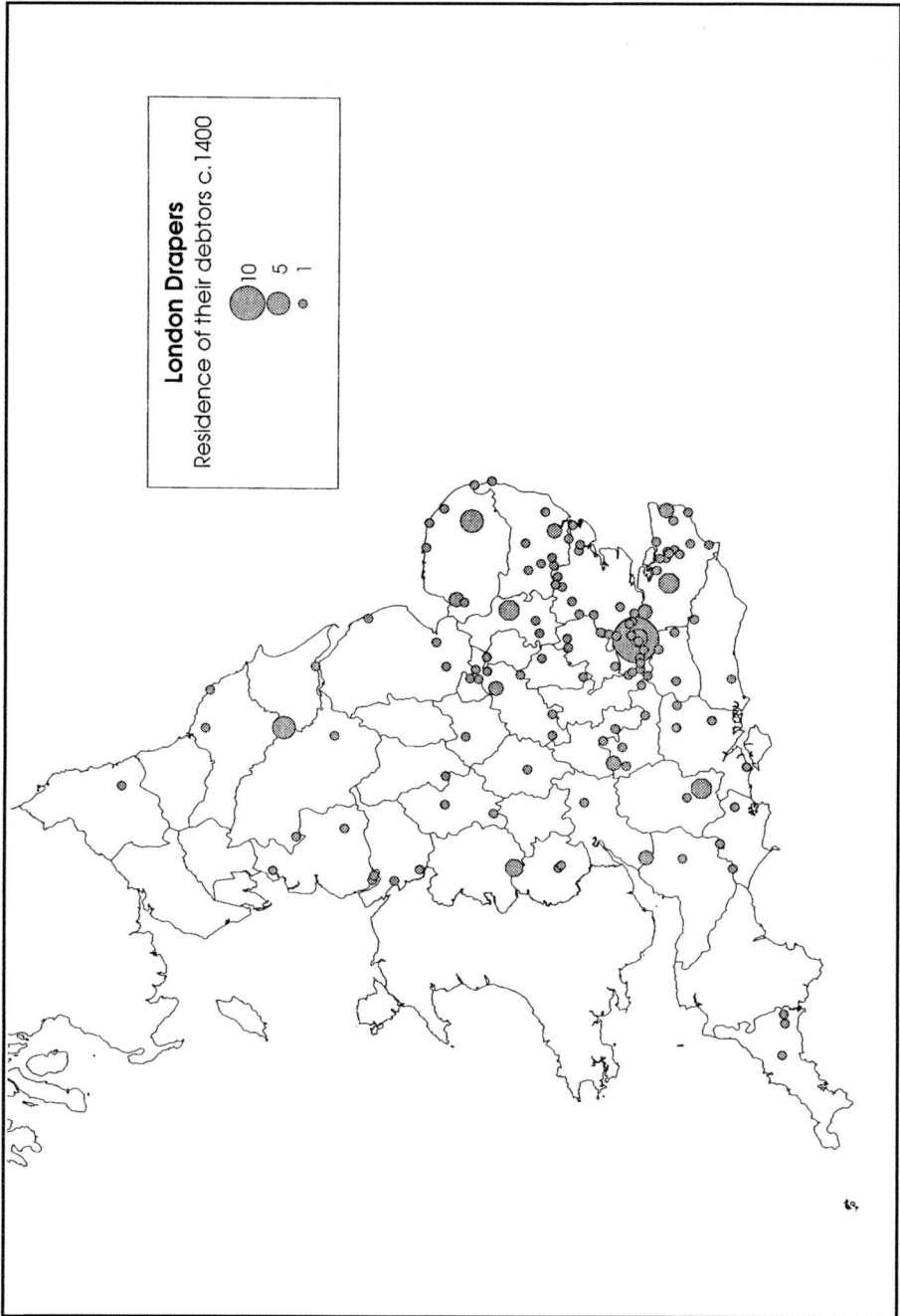

London Drapers

Residence of their debtors c.1400

10
5
1

Figure 3. Drapers' debtors c.1400

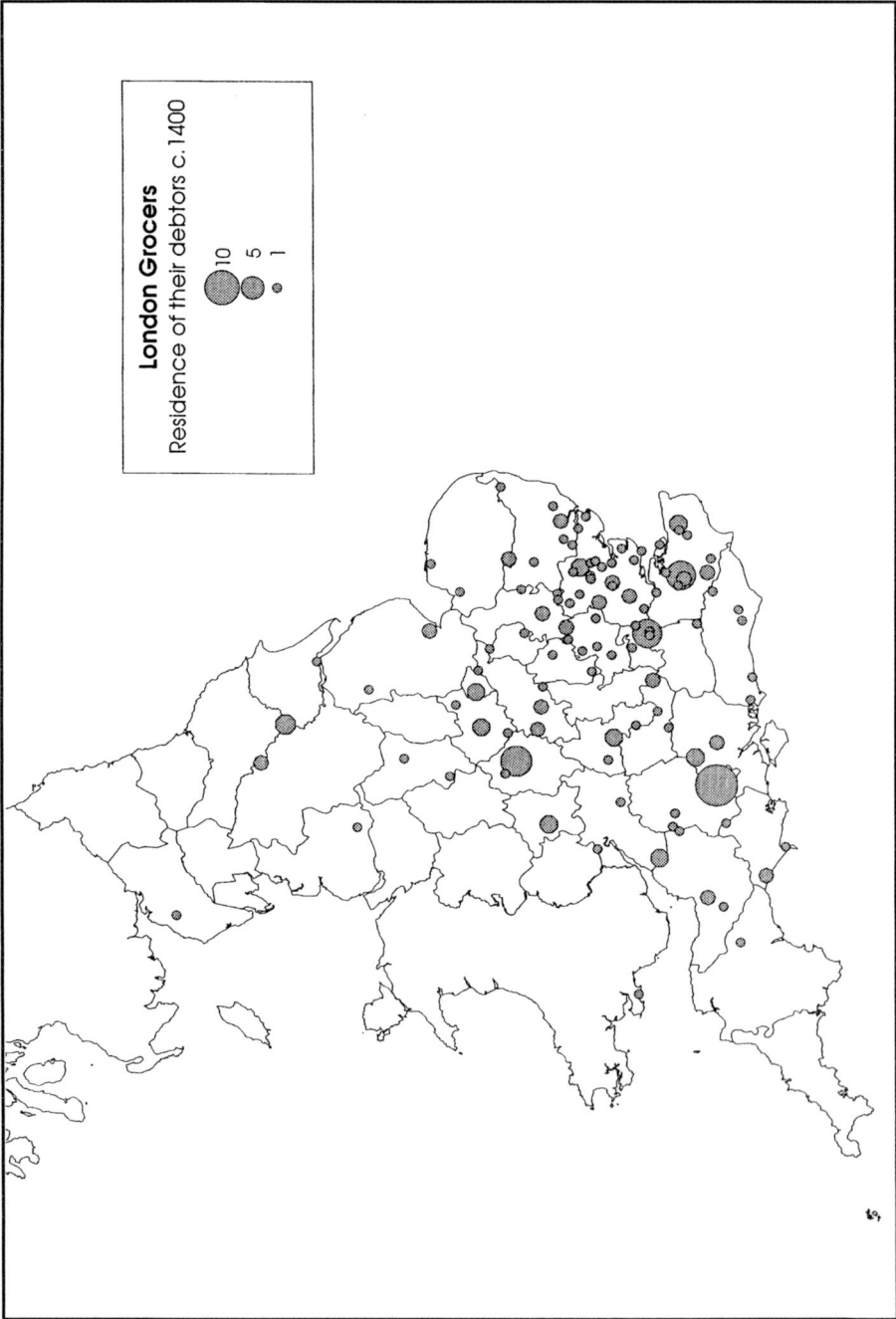

London Grocers
Residence of their debtors c.1400

10
5
1

Figure 4. Grocers' debtors c.1400

transactions at a period of scarcity of coin.[32] Among smaller towns with a concentration of grocers' debtors, Maidstone again appears prominent, in part no doubt reflecting its own significance as a centre of cloth-finishing, but perhaps more importantly reflecting its pivotal role in the trade of Kent, linking the populous countryside of central Kent, and the developing industrial areas of the Weald to the south-west, to London and the wider world via the navigable lower Medway and the Thames estuary. Two of the Maidstone debtors were spicers, suggesting wholesale supply of spice, dried fruit and other items of grocers'-ware to provincial retailers. Similar contacts are evident with a range of small and medium-sized towns, notably in Essex, where spicers in debt to London grocers occur at Halstead, Southminster, Chelmsford and Brentwood.

The group whose debtors' residences were on average most distant from London were the skinners, whose interests c.1400 still largely lay in the trade and working of skins and furs, producing high-value clothing for wealthy consumers.[33] Mapping the data shows, however, that compared to the mercers, the skinners had relatively few contacts in northern and south-western England (Figure 5) Instead, the men and women owing money to London skinners display a marked tendency to reside in the interior of the country, either to the immediate north-west of London or, more strikingly, in the west and north midlands, in a broad band running from Herefordshire north-east to Nottinghamshire, and just extending into south Yorkshire. By contrast, relatively few lived near the coast, with notably few residences in Essex and Suffolk, which feature so strongly in the hinterlands of the other companies. The explanation is not immediately apparent, but may lie in the role of provincial ports vis-à-vis London in the importation of different commodities c.1400, although the capital is known to have dominated the import trade in furs and skins by the 1390s. Certainly the skinners from elsewhere who joined the Londoners' fraternity in the fifteenth century came predominantly from inland towns such as Coventry, Leicester, Northampton and Salisbury, although the port of Boston also features, and they seem primarily to have done so in order to secure supplies of imported skins.[34] The provincial skinners who feature in the database owing money to their London counterparts came from a wider geographical area, from Saltash in Cornwall to York, but the majority were again found in inland towns to the north-west, including St Albans, Lichfield, Shrewsbury and Birmingham.

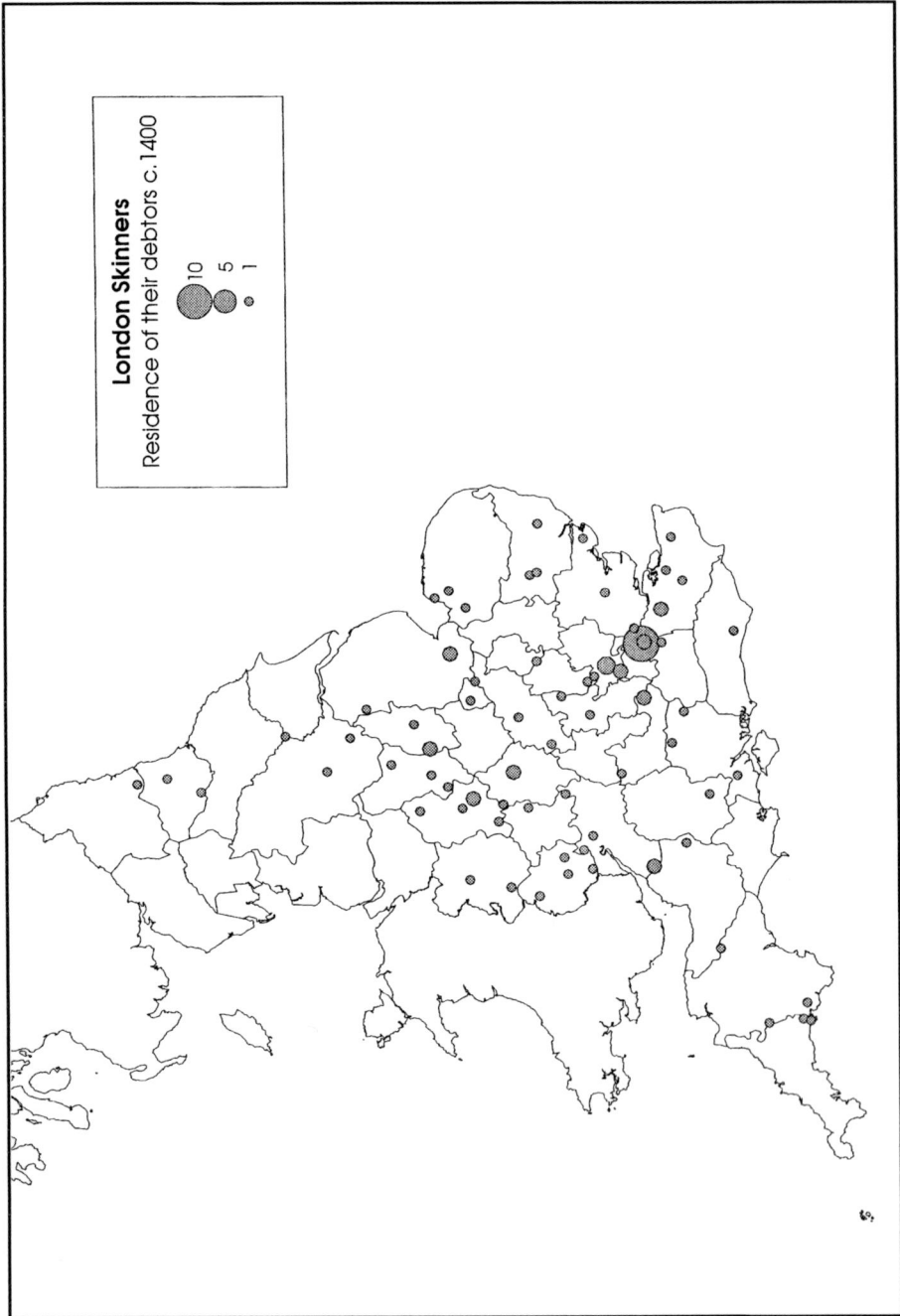

London Skinners

Residence of their debtors c.1400

10
5
1

Figure 5. Skinners' debts c.1400

By contrast, the London vintners, whose core interests lay in a valuable but relatively bulky product, seem at this date to have been less successful in breaking into the trade hinterlands served by the major provincial towns and ports than were those companies whose primary business concerned cloth, and other light and more readily transportable commodities. Southampton–well-placed to distribute a commodity arriving from the south–is known to have supplied an extensive area of south-central England with wine and other goods by overland transport, and Bristol, King's Lynn and Hull undoubtedly supplied wine to similarly extensive hinterlands by river and road.[35] Most of the vintners' debtors within the sample lived in counties immediately to the north and west of the city, with a notable group of residences in eastern Hertfordshire probably reflecting trade on the river Lea (Figure 6). Land-locked north Buckinghamshire and south Northamptonshire were home to another small cluster of debtors. Perhaps surprisingly, a few debtors also lived in Bristol and the south-west midlands. Information on debtor occupations is thinner than for the larger groupings discussed above, but appear to reflect the direct supply of wine to consumers of middling status–including clerks, craftsmen, husbandmen and yeomen–as well as some of knightly and esquire rank and (surprisingly few) provincial retailers, such as Richard Lexham, innkeeper, of Dunstable in Bedfordshire. Higher-ranking consumers at this period seem often to have arranged direct purchase and transport of wine from the ports, another factor reducing the size and geographical extent of the market for London's vintners.[36]

Conclusion

The analysis and mapping of a large body of debt litigation can thus be seen to throw considerable light on aspects of London's distributive trade in the decades around 1400. The overall extent of the city's hinterland, the contrasting sphere's of operation of the principal mercantile groups, and their characteristic modes of trading can all be examined in new and systematic ways. This paper has described the sources and methods used, and attempted some preliminary characterisation of the city's multi-layered distributive hinterland. All the issues touched upon demand fuller investigation, bearing as they do upon some of the major themes of later medieval English economic

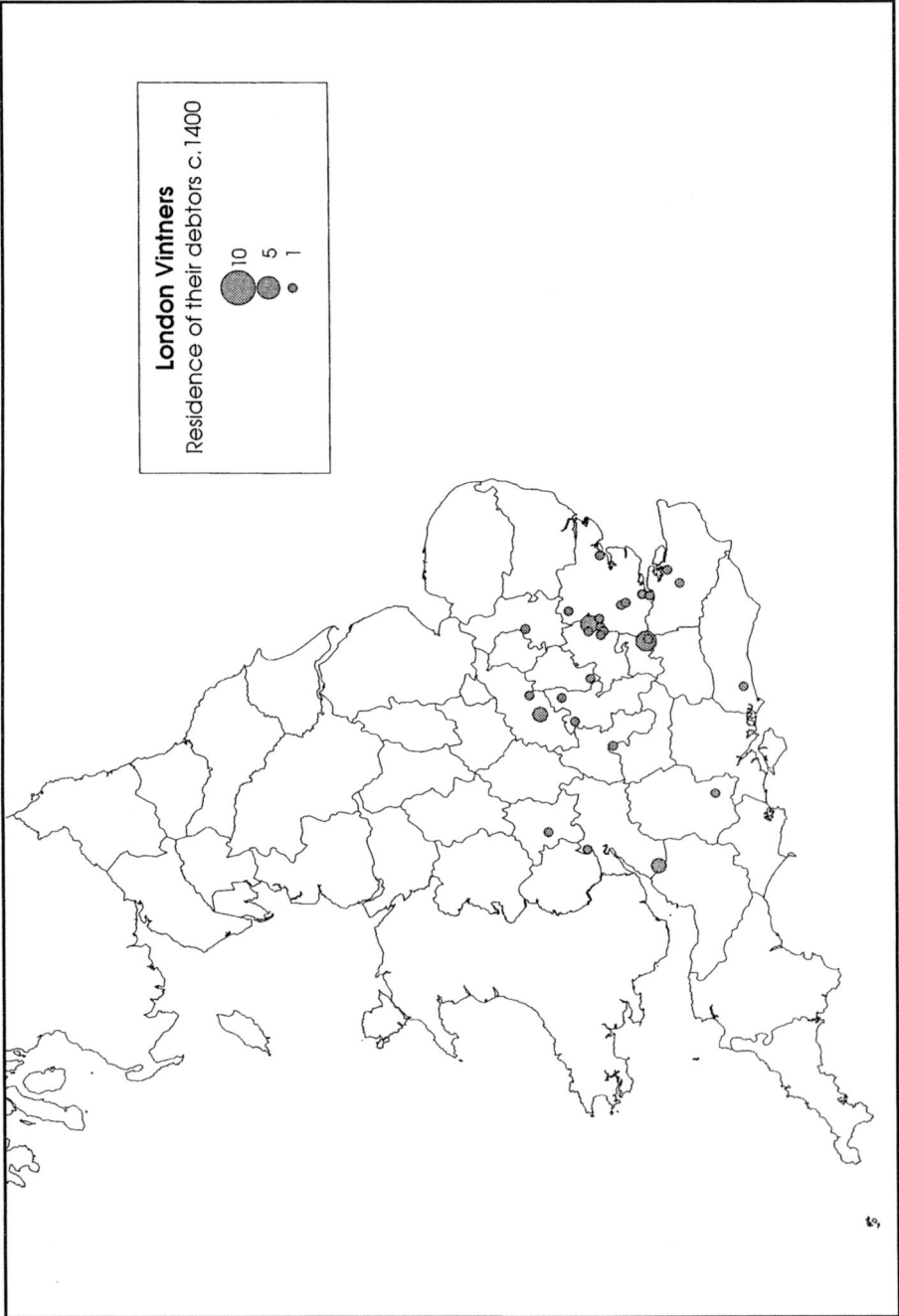

London Vintners
Residence of their debtors c.1400

10
5
1

Figure 6: Vintners' debts c.1400

history. Among the most recurrent of these themes is the economic difficulty experienced by many important towns and ports–an 'urban crisis' to some writers–and a concomitant rise in the relative wealth of London. More and more of England's trade was being channelled through the capital, as the country's overseas trade and especially its cloth exports became increasingly focused upon the markets of Bruges and then Antwerp, a trend which reached its apogee towards the middle of the sixteenth century. The pattern of imports also reflected this concentration of shipping and trade upon the Thames, with provincial ports handling smaller and smaller proportions of the total. It is clear that a large part of England's internal distributive trade was already in the hands of Londoners by c.1400, and that they were supplying consumers and middlemen across an extensive part of the country. However, some regions such as the north-west and parts of the south-west remained quite weakly integrated into the London-centred system. Some relatively accessible counties such as Norfolk also appear to have had less interaction with London than might have been predicted, which may reflect a relative success of Norwich merchants in keeping control of the trade of their immediate hinterland. It is also clear that merchants in the different London companies had quite strikingly different trading hinterlands at this period, perhaps reflecting variations in the degree of control which London exercised over different aspects of import trade, as well as contrasts in the transportability of the goods distributed. Were provincial towns declining (if they were) because Londoners were increasingly penetrating their hinterlands and stealing domestic as well as overseas trade from provincial merchants? If so, what was the chronology of this process? Were the regions in most regular contact with London and London merchants benefiting economically from that interaction, or were they in some senses being 'under-developed'–stripped of skills and control of resources by the capital? By creating datasets for earlier and later periods parallel to the one employed here for the c.1400 period, it should be possible to begin systematically to address these and related issues, and to add spatial depth to our understanding of crucial processes of change and re-structuring at work in the economy of England during the later middle ages.

NOTES

[1]   This paper is based upon my presentation at the 'Reframing metropolitan history' workshop held in June 1998, but has been updated to include the results of more recently available analyses and mapping. Some of the material presented here previously appeared in J. A. Galloway, 'Market networks: London, hinterland trade and the economy of England' in *Centre for metropolitan history, annual report 1997–8 and 10th anniversary conference Papers* (London, 1999), 44–50. Most of the data drawn upon was collected during the Leverhulme Trust-funded research project 'Market networks in the London region...c.1400', based at the Centre for Metropolitan History, Institute of Historical Research, between 1994 and 1997. I am grateful to my co-researcher on that project, Margaret Murphy, and to the director of the CMH, Derek Keene, for their comments on an earlier version of this paper.

[2]   D. Keene, 'Medieval London and its region', *London Journal,* 14 (1989), 99-111.

[3]   J. Hatcher, 'The great slump of the mid-fifteenth century', and P. Nightingale, 'The growth of London in the medieval English economy', both in R. H. Britnell and J. Hatcher, eds., *Progress and problems in medieval England: Essays in honour of Edward Miller* (Cambridge, 1996), 237–72 and 89–106.

[4]   P. Nightingale, *A medieval mercantile community: the Grocers' company in the politics and trade of London, 1000–1485* (New Haven and London, 1995).

[5]   S. Thrupp 'The grocers of London: a study of distributive trade', in E. Power and M. M. Postan, eds, *Studies in English trade in the fifteenth century* (London, 1933), 276-7.

[6]   For an overview see R. J. Johnston, *Geography and geographers: Anglo-American human geography since 1945,* 5th edn. (London, 1997).

[7]   See for example J. Langdon, *Horses, oxen and technological innovation: the use of draught animals in English farming from 1066–1500* (Cambridge, 1986); B. M. S. Campbell, 'People and land in the Middle Ages, 1066–1500' in R. A. Dodghson and R. A. Butlin, eds, *An historical geography of England and Wales,* 2nd edn. (London, 1990), 69–122; C. Dyer, 'The consumer and the market in the later middle ages', *Economic History Review,* 43 (1989), 305–27.

[8]   B. M. S. Campbell, J. A. Galloway, D. Keene and M. Murphy, *A medieval capital and its grain supply: agrarian production and distribution in the London region c.1300* (Historical Geography Research Group, Research Series 30, 1993); J. A. Galloway, D. Keene and M. Murphy, 'Fuelling the city: production and distribution of firewood and fuel in London's region, 1290–1400', *Economic History Review,* 49 (1996), 447–72.

[9]   Public Record Office (PRO), Class CP40.

[10]   The actual volume of litigation probably increased somewhat less than these figures suggest, however, as larger handwriting and more detailed enrolment reduce the average number of cases per membrane. The quality of the information provided remains high until c.1570, after which date the amount of detail on the residence and occupation of parties tends to diminish. See also C. W. Brooks, *Pettyfoggers and vipers of the Commonwealth: the 'lower branch' of the legal profession in early modern England* (Cambridge, 1986), 79–84 for other measures of the changing volume of business in the royal courts.

[11] M. Hastings, *The court of common pleas in the fifteenth century* (Cornell, 1947), 157.

[12] PRO, CP40/495, 571 & 655. For the project, see note 1 above.

[13] The counties utilised were Bedfordshire, Berkshire, Buckinghamshire, Essex, Hertfordshire, Kent, Middlesex, Northamptonshire, Oxfordshire and Surrey. The database was compiled using dBase versions IV and V.

[14] Much of the analysis and all of the mapping has been undertaken using Mapinfo and Mapinfo Professional versions 3.0.2 to 4.1.2.

[15] Of 2,242 debts in the sample where the plaintiff was specifically identified as a Londoner, 87 per cent were laid in London itself and a further 11 per cent in the immediately adjoining counties of Middlesex, Surrey, Kent and Essex. The remaining six counties of the core study area contributed just 2 per cent of the total number of debt cases involving London plaintiffs.

[16] This supplementary work was carried out during the Centre for Metropolitan History project 'Metropolitan market networks *c.*1300–1600' (ESRC Award No R000237253), the main aim of which is to trace long-term changes in London's role within the English economy.

[17] P. Nightingale, 'Monetary contraction and mercantile credit in later medieval England', *Economic History Review,* 43 (1990), 560–75; J. Kermode, 'Medieval indebtedness: the regions versus London', in N. Rogers, ed., *England in the fifteenth century,* Harlaxton Medieval Studies, IV (Stamford, 1994), 72–88. Kermode identifies an increasing share for Londoners in the overall contracting number of certificates, and speculates that the source may under-represent lower-level commercial credit.

[18] J. A. Galloway, 'Town and country in England, 1300–1570', in S. R. Epstein, ed., *Town and country in pre-modern Europe* (Cambridge, forthcoming, 2001), 106–30.

[19] Poll-tax populations taken from C. Fenwick, ed., *The poll taxes of 1377, 1379 and 1381,* part 1 (Oxford, 1998) and J. C. Russell, *British medieval population,* (Albuquerque, 1948). For a parallel distribution of debts weighted by area rather than population of counties see J.A. Galloway, 'Metropolitan market networks: London's economic hinterland in the later Middle Ages', *London and Middlesex Archaeological Society Transactions,* 50 (1999), 91-7. This and the following maps are plotted using a digitised base-map of historic (pre-1974) county boundaries originally created by Professor Marjorie McIntosh of the University of Colorado; I am grateful to Professor McIntosh for permission to use and modify her map; the boundaries shown are approximate only, and should not be taken as definitive.

[20] The most second most extensive hinterland *c.*1400 probably belonged to York, but that city's area of dense economic contacts (that is, excluding the more linear linkages associated with long-distance and international trade) hardly extended beyond Yorkshire and was patchy even within the county. This emerges from preliminary analysis of data collected during the project 'Metropolitan market networks *c.*1300–1600'.

[21] The company affiliation of Londoners at this date cannot be taken as a wholly straight-forward indicator of occupational or trade specialisation-see below.

[22]   The list, which is printed in G. Unwin, *The gilds and companies of London* (London, 1938), 370–1, was intended to represent 'all the crafts exercised in London from of old and still continuing...here set down in case it may in any wise profit the hall and Company of Brewers'. The Brewers' Company rented out their hall to other companies and associations, and the relative wealth and standing of these would obviously have been of practical interest.

[23]   Tenth position in the Brewers' list is occupied by the Ironmongers.

[24]   Thrupp, 'Grocers of London', 261ff.

[25]   Cornwall Record Office, AR37/40–5. I am grateful to Hannes Kleineke for allowing me to use his transcription of these documents.

[26]   H. Kleineke, 'The Dinham family in the later Middle Ages' (unpublished University of London Ph.D. thesis, 1998), 127; Dyer, 'Consumer and the market'.

[27]   73 per cent of those cases where both plaintiff and defendant residence were specified and the defendant was a Londoner.

[28]   The order of company affiliations has been taken from Table 2 above, but it will be seen that when only those debts where the defendant's residence is specified are counted some changes occur; e.g. drapers occur more frequently than grocers as plaintiffs (342 to 203) but more grocers' debtors than drapers' debtors had a specified place of residence (175 to 172). The difference may relate to the contrasting business profiles of the two companies (see text).

[29]   Nightingale, *Mercantile community,* 366.

[30]   Dyer, 'Consumer and the market', 309.

[31]   C. Barron, 'Centres of conspicuous consumption: the aristocratic town-house in London', *London Journal,* 20 (1995), 1–17, esp. 7–9; D. Keene, 'Wardrobes in the City: houses of consumption, finance and power', in M. Prestwich, R. Britnell and R. Frame eds, *Thirteenth-century England,* vii (Woodbridge, 1999), 61–79.

[32]   Nightingale, *Mercantile community,* 352.

[33]   E. Veale, *The English fur trade in the later middle ages* (Oxford, 1966).

[34]   Veale, *English fur trade,* 71–2.

[35]   Southampton's inland distributive trade is recorded in the fifteenth century *Brokage Books,* a number of which have been published in the Southampton Records Series (Southampton, various dates).

[36]   Dyer, 'Consumer and the market', 309–11.

Computers, maps and metropolitan London in the 1690s
Craig Spence

Introduction

This chapter describes the various uses computers were put to during the research project 'Metropolitan London in the 1690s', undertaken at the Centre for Metropolitan History between 1991–4.[1] The project delineated and explored a wide range of social and economic measures across the full extents of the metropolis. A number of the more significant measures are discussed later in this paper by way of example. Computers were central to the work from the level of data collection, through database analysis, to the graphical mapping of research findings. Throughout, the project was restricted to a PC-based platform using, for the most part, commercially available software applications; nonetheless substantial research achievements were attained. The main academic objective of the project was to describe and review the social and economic structure of the metropolis during the later seventeenth century. Particular emphasis was placed upon the London-wide nature of the research. All of London's administrative districts, where records survived, were encompassed by the study. The final results of the project were assembled into a published atlas, which itself was compiled using a DTP application to generate camera-ready-copy.[2]

London at the end of the seventeenth century was a city of just over 500,000 people. The metropolis was larger in population, though perhaps less grand in its architecture, than Paris, and competed aggressively for global economic markets with Amsterdam, its main rival as a northern European entrepôt. When compared with the capitals of other European states London can be seen to have concentrated an unparalleled volume of national trade, money and power within its boundaries. While that convergence gave London a clear and often singular identity within the national intellect, on closer inspection the metropolis was found to comprise a number of distinctive neighbourhoods, each of which had their own character and function.

The historic core of London lay in the City, an area mainly constrained by the circuit of the Roman and medieval walls. There the merchants held sway and engaged in both a vigorous commodity trade and innovatory financial undertakings. To the west of the City, just beyond the legal district, lay the West End. That area, with its modern housing and enhanced cultural opportunities, became home to many of the London-based aristocracy and to those who formed the rising professional and political élites. The ancient parish of St Margaret Westminster, to the south-west of the West End, formed a small yet perhaps even more diverse community of bishops and lords, craftworkers and criminals. To the north and east of the metropolis dwelt a somewhat lower status community of specialised manufacturers and day-labourers. Downriver from London Bridge, on both the northern and southern banks of the Thames, a large proportion of the capital's poorer inhabitants were engaged in a host of maritime related trades including shipbuilding and repair.

Developments in the administration of tax gathering during the later seventeenth century created a number of significant archival resources. Those documents provide an essential tool with which to investigate the social and economic structures that both connected and separated London's diverse population. The decade of the 1690s was a period of war. King William III was engaged in a series of expensive military campaigns for which parliament was obliged to provide funds. In order to raise the considerable sums required a number of innovative changes took place in the manner of taxation. In particular the way in which information was compiled about the tax-paying population underwent a significant transformation. Taxpayers, and their households, were recorded in a far more detailed fashion than had previously been attempted. The focus of revenue generation also changed, with taxation based upon wealth becoming a far more significant element of the process. In an attempt to maximise fiscal revenues a number of differing taxes were enacted in quick succession during that particular decade. The records associated with those taxes provide a range of historical sources that both overlap and complement each other in terms of the information they provide. The principal taxes enacted (and employed by the project) were the Poll Tax (returns for 1692), the Four Shilling Aid (assessments for 1693-4) and the Marriage Duty (assessments for 1695). The detailed operation and objectives of those taxes has been described elsewhere, suffice to say that the social and economic information that can be abstracted from the associated returns and assessments make them in many ways comparable as an historical resource to the census material of the nineteenth century.[3]

Collecting and structuring the data

The intellectual and methodological roots of the project lay in James Alexander's postgraduate work on the returns for the 1692 poll tax.[4] Using that source in combination with the 1693–4 four shilling aid assessments Alexander was able to formulate an economic profile for those members of occupational groups present within the City of London who qualified to pay the poll tax. The '1690s' project was aimed at significantly advancing that earlier study. The poll tax returns are limited in their surviving extent to the administrative boundary of the City of London. By the end of the seventeenth century, however, the vast bulk of London's population lived not in the City but in the surrounding suburbs. In order to achieve a more comprehensive picture of the social and economic structures of the metropolis the more extensive four shilling aid assessments became the preferred primary source.

The assessment books for the four shilling aids present their information in a highly structured form, arranged by taxation district whether it be a ward, precinct or parish. The documents comprise lists of named householders, and certain lodgers—where they held taxable amounts of personal wealth—together with the tax charge based upon the rack-rent value of their property (4s. for every £1 of rent value). A further tax charge upon the value of any profits generated by their stocks or business wealth (at a rate of 24s. on every £100) was also levied. Stocks could take the form of money, stock-in-trade, goods, merchandise, paper investments or debts owing, but household goods were excluded. Occasionally the landlord of the property concerned was noted, as was a variety of other information. Non-household property, most frequently stables, shops, warehouses, wharves and the like, were often expressly cited. The only significant restriction was that tax was not to be levied on property where rents fell below a yearly minimum of £1, a relatively rare event in the case of London.

Local inhabitants of sound reputation were selected by parliamentary appointed commissioners to gauge their neighbours' rents and wealth and so set the levels of tax owed. Such valuations were, therefore, often made on the basis of personal knowledge and are considered to be a relatively accurate guide to actual levels of rent and wealth. Collection of the aids was also very efficient—the cash book of the chamberlain of the City of London indicates that 98.5 per cent of the £300,734 of assessed revenue for London, Westminster and the County of Middlesex was actually collected.[5] That assessment figure indicates that in real terms the cities of London and Westminster, and the county of Middlesex had a combined rental and assessable stock (or wealth) value of around £4,760,000.

As noted above the data from the four shilling aid assessments were compiled and analysed using computers. Data-entry was conducted in the archive when well-structured assessments were encountered, while more complex assessments were transcribed and entered into the database only after an initial editorial review. The database application chosen at the outset of the project was dBase IV, a relatively unsophisticated relational database package but which allowed data interrogation through SQL queries. The structure of the main database table was designed to resemble closely the organisation of the original assessment documents. The primary structuring element of the assessments, and hence the primary key for the entered data, was that of location. Assessment books, which ranged from a single sheet of some twenty names to a ninety-eight page book of more than 3,000 entries, were compiled by assessors working within particular parishes or City wards.[6] Within each document intra-divisional areas—precincts, parishes or parochial wards—were used to group the runs of individual valuations. The use of street and alley names as headings within the lists of taxpayers often indicated the progress of the assessors as they perambulated the streets of their particular district. As each entry represented a householder, or wealthy lodger within that house or household, the collated locational information could be used to provide a unique geo-locational attribute for each database record.

Given the range of civic, fiscal, and parochial geographic entities employed by the army of metropolitan assessors the various locational attributes were identified using a four-part code. Encoding overcame any problems that may have arisen in attempting to rank assessment areas by using contemporary definitions. Encoding was also useful where similar types of area, for example parishes, were employed by the assessors at differing structural levels during the compilation of assessment documents. At its highest level the code indicated a City ward or a metropolitan parish, which usually equated to a single assessment document. Below that level intra-divisional areas were indicated, such as parochial wards or precincts, followed by street or alley names (when the particular side of a street was cited it was assigned a separate code but at the same hierarchical level). The final element in the code was a series of consecutive numbers related to individual household entries; a subsidiary numeric code used to indicate wealthy lodgers ensured that the completed locational code formed a unique primary key for each record, see Table 1. This system, in the majority of cases, allowed the rapid geo-locational identification of individual households within the overall database.

Metropolitan parish or City ward	Intra-divisional area (ward, division, parish, precinct)	Street, alley, yard, etc. (and side)	Household(er)	Associated householder or lodger
nn/	nn/	nnn/	nnnn	.n
Example				
34	02	001	0011	.1
St Paul Covent Garden	West Division	Henrietta Street South	Mrs Susannah Ball	Mrs Susannah Ball
34	02	001	0011	.2
St Paul Covent Garden	West Division	Henrietta Street South	Mrs Susannah Ball	Charles Bates esq

Table 1. The structure of the locational coding field within the four shilling aid database

The names and titles of householders, their landlords, and their occupation if mentioned were entered within relevant character fields. The assessed taxation values were decimalised then entered into numeric fields. After the period of data-capture and following critical examination of the collected data a small number of additional fields were added to the database table structure. Those fields, for example, helped to indicate the number of households that each record specifically referred to or the gender of each named taxpayer. The additional fields were extremely useful during the data analysis phase in allowing rapid calculation of certain values; this was particularly important when grouping results by gender. In addition a subsidiary dataset was abstracted from the main database and held in a separate table to provide more detailed information on non-household property, such as stables, breweries, shops, warehouses and the like.

In total 61,588 unique records were entered into the main database. The assessments supplied 53,250 named entries for rent taxpayers, primarily householders, and 20,643 named entries for stock taxpayers, of the latter figure 3,789 appeared to have been lodgers. Significant additional information concerning household structure—wives, children, servants, apprentices and kin—and occupational attributions for 17,565 taxpayers resident within the City of London was contributed from a further database compiled from the 1692 poll tax returns. Similar material, including personal names of household members, was obtained from the assessments collected for the 1695 marriage duty.[7]

Mapping the data

A primary objective of the '1690s' project was the geographical analysis of metropolitan society and the subsequent graphical representation of those results in published form. Given the size of the database and the extents of metropolitan London in the later seventeenth century computer based mapping seemed particularly appropriate. A number of steps had to be taken to structure geographically the social and economic data (partly described above) and also to provide a suitable digital base-map on which to situate the research results. It was, however, necessary first to ascertain what might have constituted a contemporary perception of the extent of metropolitan London.

Reference was made to the list of parishes found printed within the *Bills of Mortality* for the 1690s as these were considered to provide a general, though not entirely complete, picture of contemporary metropolitan identity.[8] The *Bills* indicate that 134 parishes were then considered to have been part of the metropolitan area. Among the districts regarded as representing the metropolis were the City of London, the city of Westminster and a large part of both urban and rural Middlesex and Surrey. Four shilling aid assessments survive for all those areas north of the River Thames, however no assessments survive for areas south of the River.[9]

There is a major disadvantage in using parochial areas, or for that matter City wards, to aggregate social and economic data within the metropolitan context. London parishes are not good units of analysis as they do not have regular shapes and they encompass a great variation in population numbers (see Figure 1). An urban parish within the City of London, for example, may have had as few as twenty households while a semi-rural parish in Middlesex or Westminster might contain as many as three thousand. Such differences can be resolved statistically or spatially using techniques such as cluster analysis, however in this instance it was felt that a more direct map-based solution would be most appropriate. Consequently a new set of natural, or coherent, analytical area boundaries were formulated with the intention that each area would hold an equivalent number of households.

The new boundaries were constructed with reference to the detailed locational information found within the four shilling aid assessments themselves; the same information used to assign the locational coding as outlined above. In particular it was possible to adjust the new boundaries in specific areas by making reference to street names and to yards and alleyways that tended to represent small yet coherent groups of households. The resulting analytical areas were constructed with a view to functional unity, respecting both topographic and economic elements of the metropolitan structure, and in this way helping to provide greater visual regularity (see Figure 2). Through the detailed manipulation of those boundaries each area was equally weighted with a mean population of 450 households.[10] Thus when mapped the various social and economic measures had a visual integrity that would have been poorly served if a statistical redistribution had been applied to the parochial populations, and had the existing boundaries been retained.

In order to digitise both the boundaries of the contemporary assessments districts and those of the newly formulated analytical areas it was necessary to construct a digital base-map of late seventeenth century London. Three major contemporary maps were used to provide the information upon which such a base-map could be constructed:

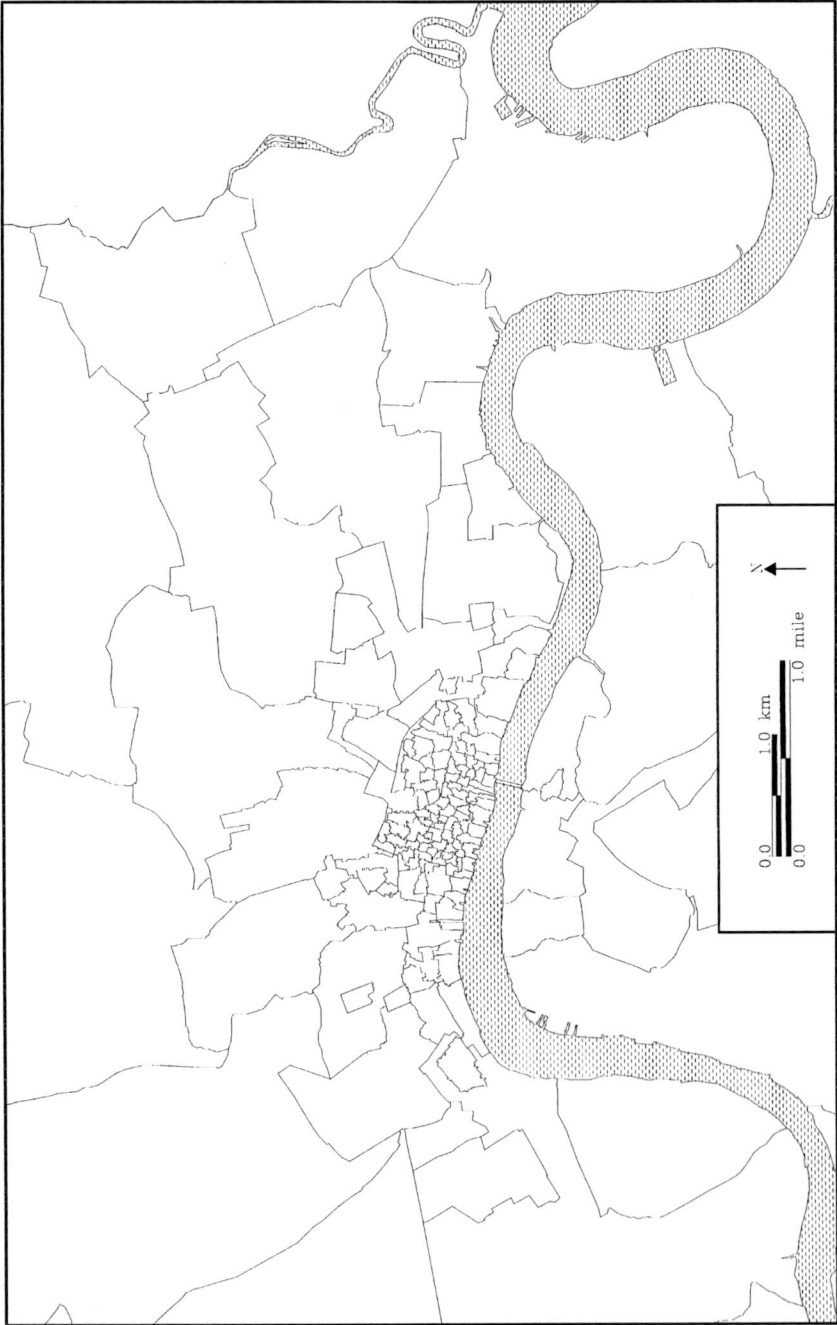

Figure 1. Parish boundaries in metropolitan London, c.1700

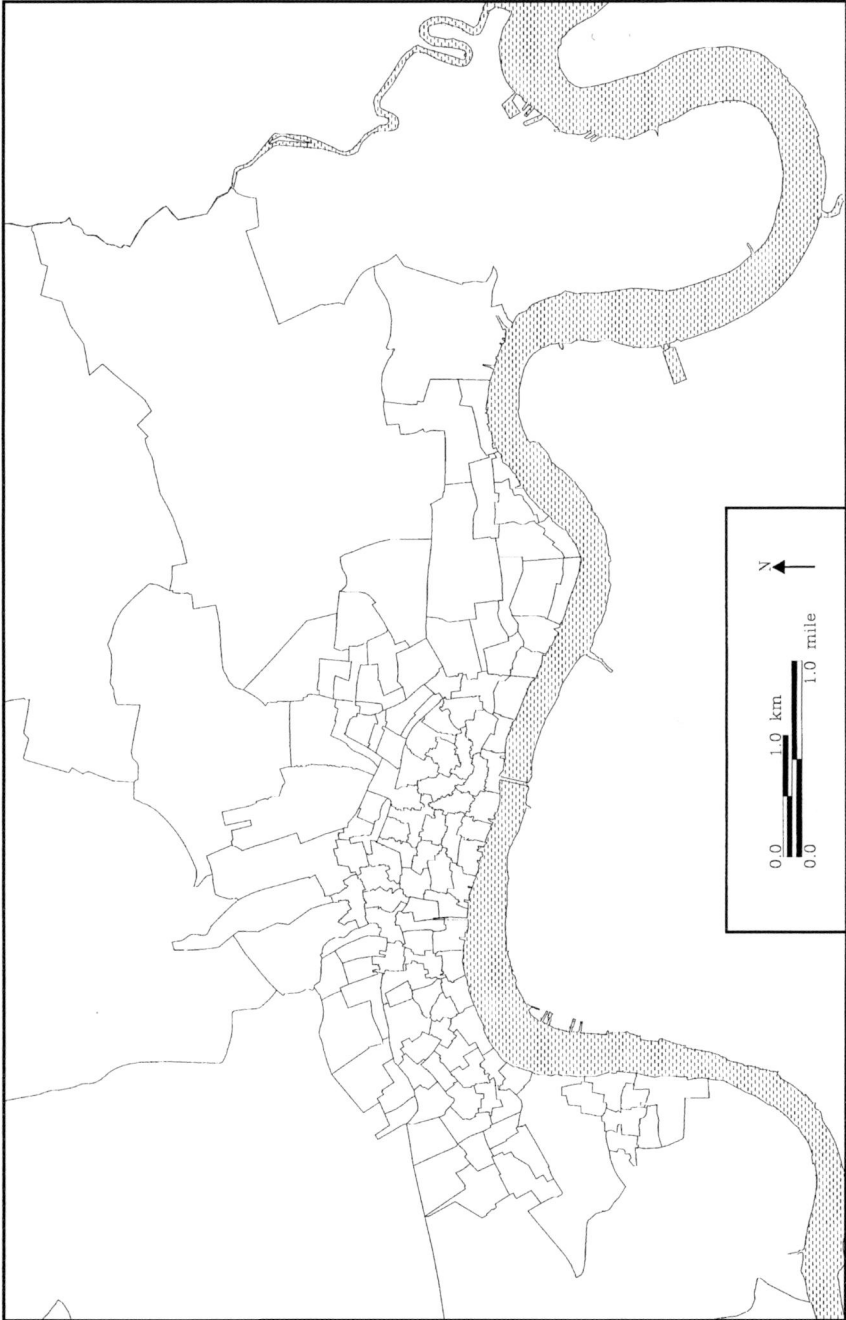

Figure 2. Boundaries of the newly formulated 450-household analytical areas

0.0   1.0 km

0.0   1.0 mile

N

Morgan's map of the City and Westminster dated to 1682, the parish maps printed in Strype's *Survey of London* published in 1755, though surveyed at a somewhat earlier date (probably between 1708–20), and Rocque's map of the entire built-up area of London in 1746. Those and other local maps were used to define the boundaries of the various assessment districts as they were during the 1690s and also to establish the topographic background for the study area, in particular the road network.

The quality and detail of seventeenth and eighteenth century maps is both varied and unpredictable, furthermore none meet modern surveying criteria for accuracy. In order to attain a more accurate representation of the metropolis the first rigorously surveyed maps of London–the Ordnance Survey Maps of the 1860s–were selected to provide a 'foundation' for the construction of the base-map. The Ordnance Survey maps were meticulously surveyed but also importantly pre-date most of the nineteenth century metropolitan street improvements. The mapping process entailed the careful identification of each boundary, using a variety of both textual and visual sources, followed by delineation of the course of the boundary on copies of the principal contemporary maps. Finally those boundaries were translated onto a base-map of the late-seventeenth century street plan, produced with direct reference to those streets depicted on the Ordnance Survey maps.

All sets of boundaries–parish, ward and analytical–were digitised using a vector-based package called PC-ISIS. That application accepted data-entry via a large-format digitising tablet. The digitising process used arbitrarily located poly-centres to identify polygon interiors and accurately plotted boundary nodes to fix the extents of the polygon; the boundaries themselves were recorded as shared segments running from one node to the next. The road network was entered as a set of key nodes joined by segment links to form a network. Graphical analysis of attribute data was undertaken using a PC-based mapping application called QuickMap. The QuickMap application–based in part on the GIMMS programme–was developed and distributed by the Geography Department of University College London. Though heavily reliant on full screen menus it was a useful analytical tool during the early 1990s when there were very few affordable PC-based mapping applications on the market.[11]

QuickMap allowed a wide range of attribute data, mainly derived from SQL-based analysis of the four shilling aid database, to be integrated with the digitised boundary information. The package allowed both colour and monochrome (shaded) choropleth maps to be generated using a variety of classificatory systems. A high volume of draft maps were produced, and where appropriate such maps were exported as DXF graphics exchange files. Subsequently the maps were cleaned, edited, given ancillary detail and key orientation overlays through the use of a simple multiple layer CAD (drawing) package. The selected application was AutoSketch, a cheap PC-based programme that allowed a number of important refinements to be made to the draft maps. Using the CAD package a selection of the maps were brought to a high enough graphical standard to make possible their inclusion as Camera-Ready-Copy within the published atlas.

On completion of the research phase of the project a version of the four shilling aid database, as originally transcribed, was fully documented and submitted to the History Data Service at the University of Essex.[12] In a similar manner a copy of the digital boundary map for London's parishes, as they were around 1700, was submitted to the 'Great Britain Historical GIS Project' based at the University of Portsmouth. The major research outcomes have been published as *London in the 1690s: A Social Atlas*. The atlas reviews a significant range of the structural elements of the metropolis—physical topography, transport infra-structure, land use and the like—and also presents the main social and economic findings of the project. By way of illustration a selection of the research findings are outlined below.

Some results

The most straightforward element of the analysis was the establishment of mean rent values for the metropolitan area. The London-wide mean value for residential rent during the decade of the 1690s was found to have been £17 3s. p.a. The highest value residential property was, however, Burlington House on Piccadilly, which exhibited a rent of £320 p.a. The pattern of rent values across the metropolis was mapped using nested means and is shown in Figure 3. The map shows two central high-value districts, in the City and along the Strand (with a joint mean of £36 2s. p.a.). There was a further element

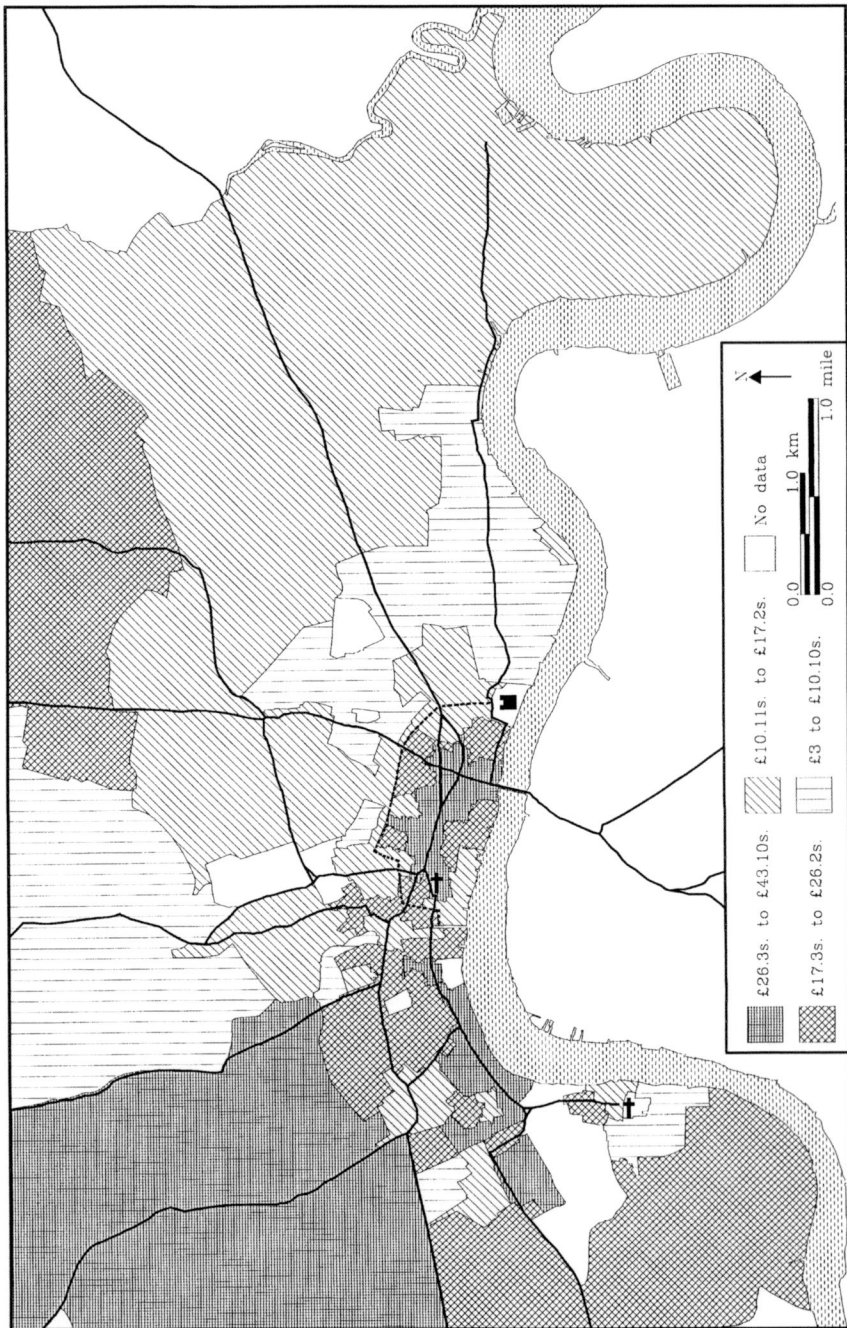

Figure 3. Mean household rent value per annum
Source: 1693–4 Aid database.

Legend:
- £26.3s. to £43.10s.
- £17.3s. to £26.2s.
- £10.11s. to £17.2s.
- £3 to £10.10s.
- No data

Scale:
- 0.0 — 1.0 km
- 0.0 — 1.0 mile

N

of the high-value pattern in the area around St James' Square, south of Piccadilly (£34 8s. p.a.).

Those districts with mean values less than £10 10s. were found almost exclusively to the east of the City. In Spitalfields and Aldgate poor quality, densely situated housing was likely to have been associated with an extensive array of low-value rents. Similar environments and rents were also found in St Margaret Westminster and around Saffron Hill at approximately £5 p.a.

Using topographical data, some of which was generated automatically by QuickMap from the digitised base-map, together with the rental analysis it was possible to establish two further important measures, land values and household densities. By calculating the aggregated value of all rents for each hectare within the analytical areas it was possible to determine the broad variation in land values across the metropolis in terms of rent per hectare.

The mean value of land within the contiguous built-up area of London was just over £2,073 per hectare (£840 per acre). Despite this relatively high figure a great variety of land values were displayed across the wider extents of the metropolitan area. These ranged from £11/ha (£4/acre) in the eastern semi-rural parishes of Bromley-by-Bow, Poplar and Blackwall, up to £5,700/ha (£2,306/acre) for the central commercial district of Cornhill.[13] When those values were mapped a more clearly concentric pattern is discernible, especially if compared with that of mean rent (Figure 3). The areas of highest value were associated in the main with busy commercial and retailing districts extending along major roads. A further area of high value was the riverside district immediately east of London Bridge. There the mean value of £3,950/ha (£1,599/acre) was undoubtedly associated with lucrative levels of merchant activity and the handling of international trade.

The pattern established in Figure 4 indicates a model in which land values fell with increased distance from the centres of business, though a range of other factors relating to the particular character of districts contributed to the establishment of the value of any given area. One such additional factor was that of household density. In order to refine the figures for household density simple measures of area were re-calculated using net-residential area. Such a measure eliminates those intra-urban areas that could not have had a residential function, such as markets, squares, tenter-grounds, and the like. While the total area of the

Figure 4. Land value in rack-rent pounds per hectare
Source: 1693–4 Aid database

£ 2,028 to £ 5,699

£ 1,489 to £ 2,028

£ 797 to £ 1,489

£ 361 to £ 797

£ 11 to £ 361

No data

N

1.0 km

1.0 mile

0.0

0.0

built-up extents of the metropolis was in the region of 920 hectares (2,300 acres) the measure of net residential area for the same extents amounted to the smaller figure of some 740 hectares (1,830 acres).[14] Using that measure the mean household density for the metropolitan area was calculated as 85 households per hectare. While in general the highest household densities were found toward the centre of the metropolis and the lowest on the periphery, unlike land values the pattern was not a simple concentric one (Figure 5). The pattern was in fact found to have been at its least uniform in those areas of highest density.

Two explanations for areas of high density can be suggested. First, that poorer areas on the periphery contained both high densities of very small houses and many cases of multiple occupancy. For example the precinct of St Katherine by the Tower had an extremely high density of 185 households/ha. Alternatively, and in sharp social and economic contrast, some central areas with very similar densities, might be explained by the intense commercial pressures that were exerted on central urban space. For example, such areas included the exceedingly commercial neighbourhood of the Royal Exchange and Cornhill (112 households/ha).

To the west of the City in the West End some similar patterns can be identified. However, the two high density concentrations to the north of that area, in the northern half of St James and around Lambs Conduit Fields (120 households/ha), are harder to explain. It is however possible that they represent areas of newer buildings constructed in a more intensive manner. It is also probable that such new buildings on the periphery of the built-up area were subject to a degree of multiple occupancy from the start.

Investigation of the database also supplied information related to patterns of social hierarchy, for example it was possible to analyse the distribution of householders by their gender (Figure 6). What is immediately striking about the map showing the percentage of households headed by women is the relative absence of such households within the central part of the City of London. Within the area extending from London Bridge to Cornhill women headed no more than 8.5 per cent of all households, that against a metropolitan mean for women householders of 14.7 per cent. The traditional male domination of the City's commercial environment and the more capital-intensive nature of residency within that area probably go some way toward

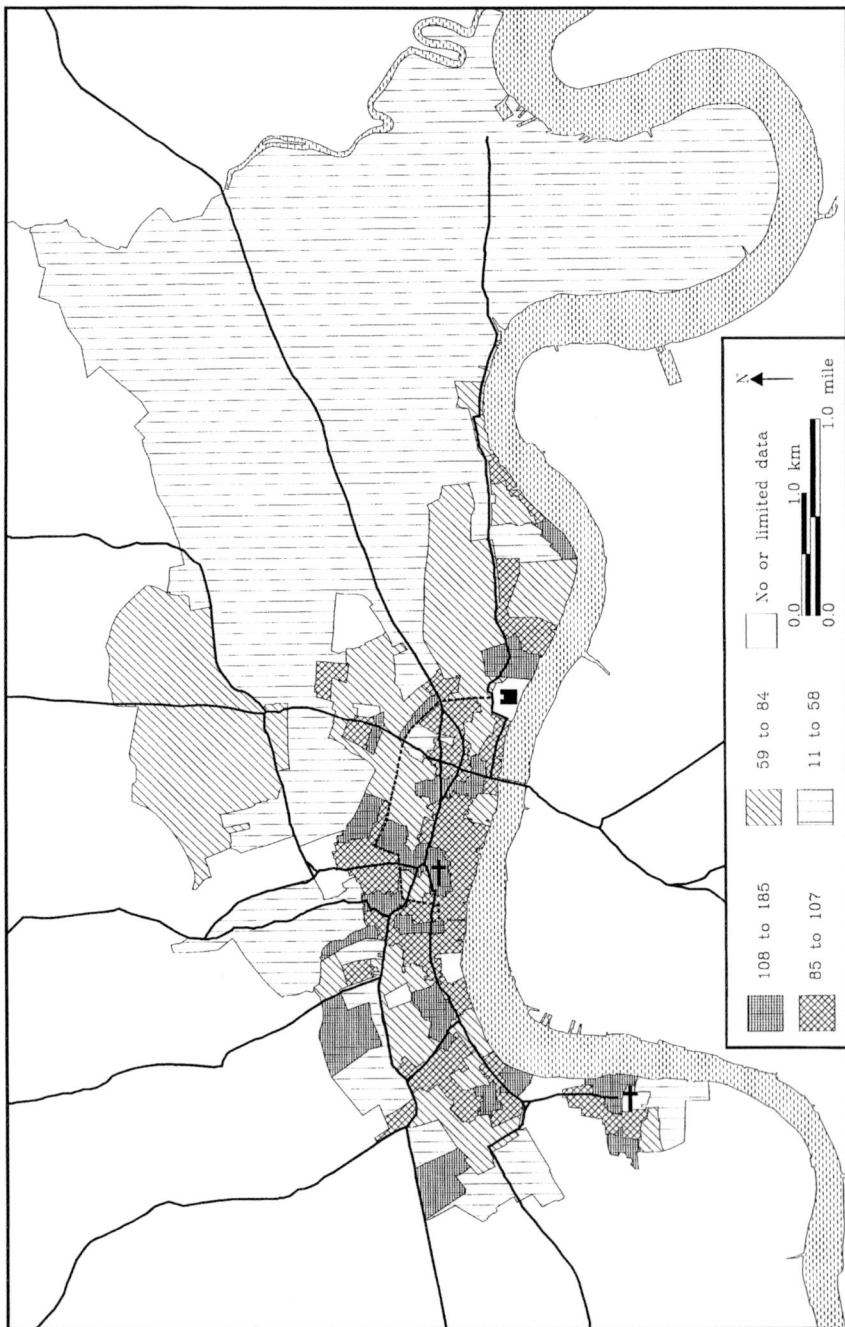

Figure 5. Household density in households per residential hectare
Source: 1693–4 Aid database

Legend:
- 108 to 185
- 59 to 84
- No or limited data
- 85 to 107
- 11 to 58

0.0 — 1.0 km
0.0 — 1.0 mile

explaining this pattern. The single district to be most heavily populated by male householders was the central area of Cheapside, near Honey Lane market, where only 5.6 per cent of all householders were women.

Nonetheless, women were found in higher than average numbers in several other districts. The highest percentage of women householders was in the northern part of the hamlet of Ratcliffe, to the east of the City, where women headed just over a quarter of all households (26.2 per cent). Other areas with high percentages were found slightly nearer the City in poor eastern districts such as the precinct of St Katherine by the Tower and around Goodmans Fields (22.8 per cent). A number of explanations might be offered to account for those high percentages and one starting point would be to consider not the presence of women as householders but the absence of a male head of household. In the eastern riverside parishes, and particularly in the hamlet of Ratcliffe, many men were employed in maritime activities and it is likely that such individuals were often absent from home, inevitably leaving their wives solely responsible for the household. Men could, however, be absent on a more permanent basis and the distribution of widows sheds some significant light on the subject.

Widows are shown as a percentage of all women householders in Figure 7. Overall widows comprised just under half of all female householders (48 per cent). What is significant about the distribution of such women is the high numbers of widows in those areas that demonstrated low percentages of women as householders. As the mapped distribution shows the City stood out as an area where if women headed a household they were very frequently widows. This can be interpreted as a further indication of the underlying male dominance of property holding within this particular area of the metropolis, even if the men involved were dead. The eastern parishes also had a high percentage of widows as householders, possibly a reflection of the dangers to both body and health that maritime employment presented to their spouses. The very low numbers of widows recorded in the West End may, however, be indicative of an area where women had access to a more independent lifestyle, or at least chose not to use or perhaps need the title 'widow'.

These are only a few of the many approaches that have been taken in analysing the 1690s database material. While the project and the published atlas have very much focused upon providing a

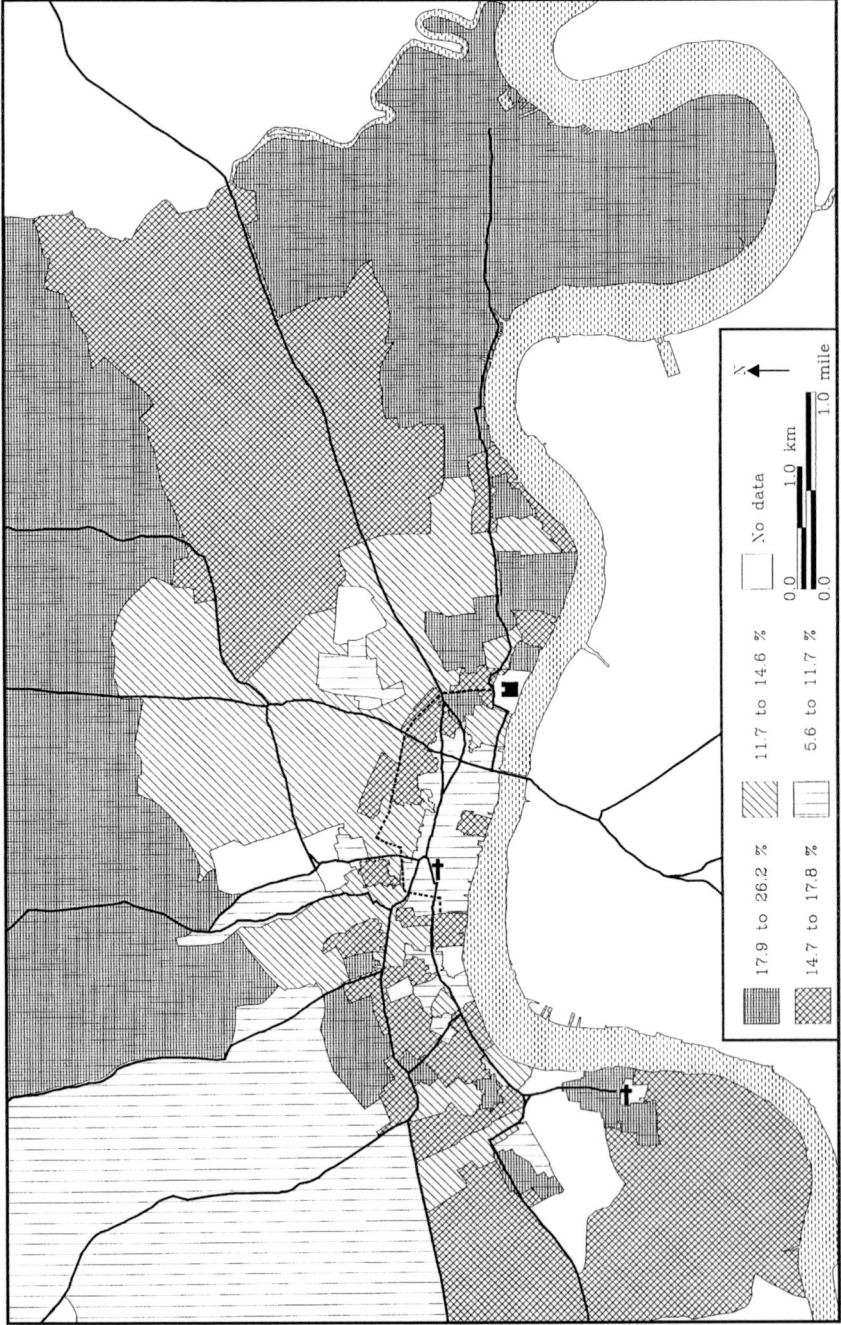

Figure 6. Percentage of households headed by women

Source: 1693–4 Aid database

Legend:
- 17.9 to 26.2 %
- 14.7 to 17.8 %
- 11.7 to 14.6 %
- 5.6 to 11.7 %
- No data

0.0   1.0 km

0.0   1.0 mile

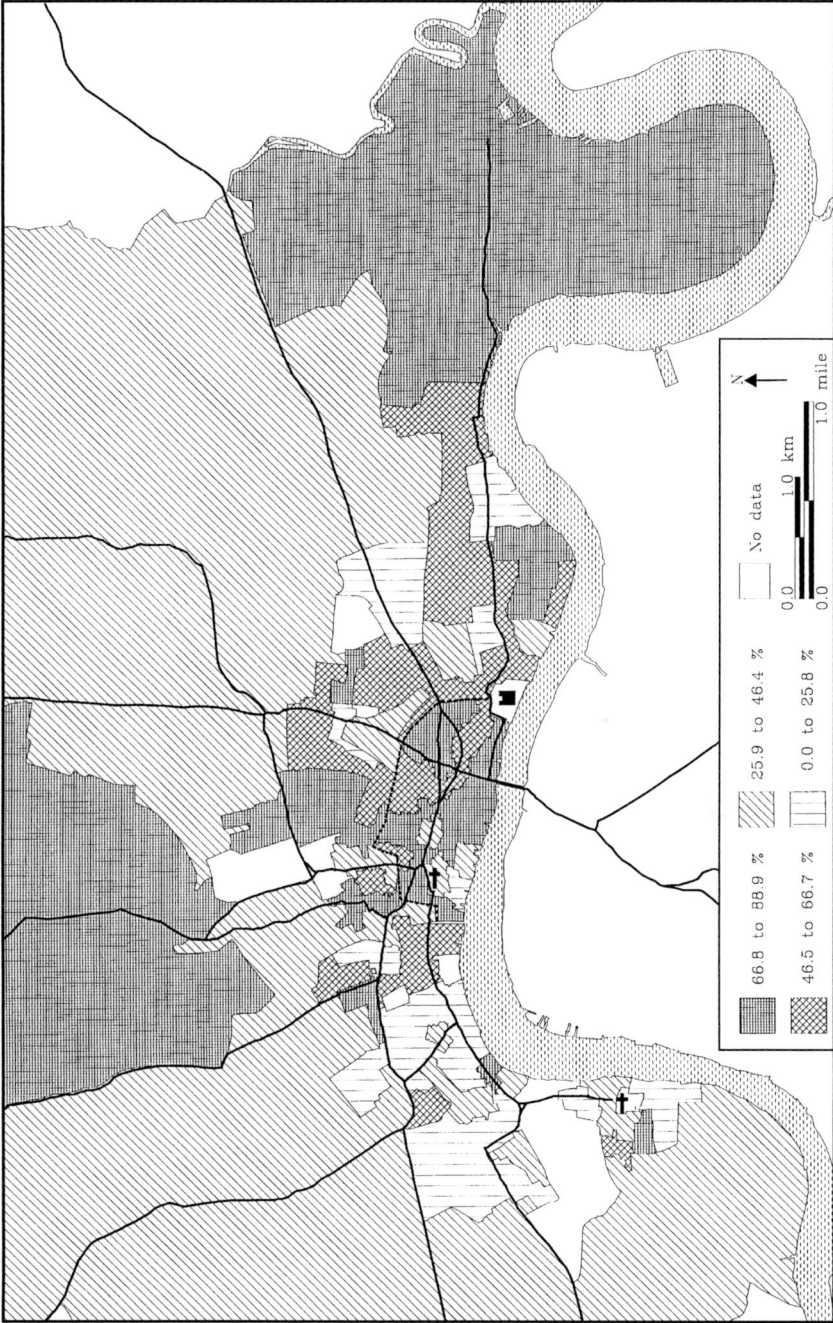

Figure 7. Percentage of female householders who were widows
Source: 1693–4 Aid database

Legend:
- 66.8 to 88.9 %
- 46.5 to 66.7 %
- 25.9 to 46.4 %
- 0.0 to 25.8 %
- No data

N

0.0   1.0 km
0.0   1.0 mile

comprehensive background picture, both the contents of the database and the various methodological developments outlined above should be of great utility for future research. Such research is most likely to follow two principal paths, firstly that of a broad comparative nature, particularly between London and other European cities. But also, and conversely, it might take a much more detailed focus, that is through the study of specific metropolitan neighbourhoods, further elucidating their social and economic characters, either during the period of the 1690s or over a somewhat longer time span. The project results themselves also raise a number of specific questions that would benefit from further study, to give just three examples;

- What were the structures of private landlordship and multiple-occupancy across the West End.

- What status did the female householder have in London and how did it differ across the extents of the metropolis.

- What underlay the finer patterns of social and economic residency in relation to occupation.

The technical methodology of the research has identified a novel way in which problems associated with comparative analysis of attribute data grouped within disparate types of contemporary boundaries can be overcome. The redistribution of such data into new natural or analytical areas can be quickly achieved using suitable RDMS/mapping software. Yet the necessary delineation of the original pre-modern boundaries on a suitable digital map-base remains both a challenging and time-consuming process.

NOTES

[1]　The project was carried out at the Centre for Metropolitan History, Institute of Historical Research, University of London. Funding was provided by the UK Economic and Social Research Council (ESRC), Grant No. R000232527.

[2]　C. Spence, London in the 1690s: a social atlas (London, 2000).

[3]　See K. Schürer and T. Arkell, Surveying the people: the interpretation and use of documentary sources for the study of population in the later seventeenth century (Oxford, 1992).

[4]　J. Alexander, 'The economic and social structure of the city of London, c.1700' (unpublished University of London Ph.D. thesis, 1989) and J. Alexander, 'The economic structure of the City of London at the end of the seventeenth century', Urban History Yearbook (1989), 47–62.

[5]   Corporation of London Record Office (CLRO), Assessment Box 40, no. 61.

[6]   All the four shilling aid assessments used by the project are held by the CLRO.

[7]   D. V. Glass, *London inhabitants within the walls, 1695,* London Record Society, 2 (1966).

[8]   Copies of the London *Bills of Mortality* for the 1690s are held by the Wellcome Institute for the History of Medicine (msl/coll/Lon).

[9]   Four shilling aid assessments are extant for all metropolitan areas north of the Thames except; the hamlet of Mile End New Town, two divisions of St Giles without Cripplegate (Golden Lane and Glasshouse Yard, and Old Street), the Artillery Ground division of Tower Liberty, Whitehall, The Temple and Lincolns Inn. The nine *Bills of Mortality* parishes south of the River Thames were; Christ Church Surrey, St George in Southwark, St Mary at Lambeth, St Mary Magdelan Bermondsey, St Mary Newington, St Mary Rotherhithe, St Olave in Southwark, St Saviour in Southwark and St Thomas in Southwark. As stated no four shilling aid assessments survive for those parishes.

[10] The majority of the areas held household numbers in the range of 350 to 650, however the following analytical areas in particular deviated from this norm; St Sepulchre, Middlesex with 263 households, St Giles Without Cripplegate, both extant liberties with 782 households, St Marylebone and St Pancras with 227 households, St Katherine by the Tower with 839 households, part of St Botolph Aldgate and Wapping Whitechapel with 729 households and Tower Liberty Intra with 2 households. These extreme values were generally the result of non-divisible administrative units. After the removal of these six values from the listing of household numbers by analytical area the following mean was calculated, 449.94 households.

[11] For a more detailed description of the use of QuickMap within the '1690s' project see, C. Spence, 'Mapping London in the 1690s', in F. Bocchi and P. Denley, eds, *Storia & multimedia: proceedings of the seventh international congress of the Association for History and Computing* (Bologna, 1994), 746–56.

[12] Copies of the four shilling aid and poll tax databases are also held by the Centre for Metropolitan History, Institute of Historical Research, University of London.

[13] The gross land value for metropolitan London was just over one tenth of the total land value of England (approx. £8,280,000). Spitalfields had the lowest value for any part of built-up area at £462/ha (£187/acre).

[14] These figures refer to the contiguous built-up area north of the River Thames.

The epidemiological implications of reconstructing hospital catchment areas in Victorian London

Graham Mooney

Epidemiological historians wishing to describe and explain spatial patterns of mortality and health in nineteenth-century England and Wales are confronted with an array of complex methodological obstacles. For example, changes in cause of death classification present a dilemma for the analysis of long-term change in particular disease groups, while temporal and geographical differences in medical diagnosis and certification are equally troublesome. Although caution must therefore be exercised when interpreting nineteenth-century cause of death statistics, the general consensus among medical historians is that such data nevertheless retain their intrinsic value.[1] Another realm of concern relates to the paucity of systematically collected information regarding morbidity and sickness that did not result in death. This lacuna hinders debate surrounding the 'health transition' in this period, during which infectious diseases declined and chronic ailments began to predominate. Yet some progress has been made recently in evaluating the incidence of non-fatal illnesses in Friendly Society records and an altogether clearer picture is beginning to emerge.[2] Meanwhile, shifting administrative boundaries make it extremely difficult to ensure that the data that is available always relates to the same geographically defined space. Technical advances and the increasing use of Geographical Information Systems are gradually reducing the scale of this problem. Finally, while the vexed and intricate question of institutional mortality has long been acknowledged by those interested in metropolitan epidemiology, neither a satisfactory nor a comprehensive solution has yet been achieved.

Interpretations of epidemiological change in the various districts of London are complicated by the fact that although many of the patients and paupers that died in institutions came from other parts of London and beyond the capital, all such deaths were counted in the mortality total of the registration district in which the institution was located. Thus, the presence of one or many large institutions in a district—hospitals, workhouses and lunatic asylums—served to inflate the death rate of that district. The purpose of this paper is to outline the steps taken towards a solution to this problem so that the picture of mortality change in the capital is rendered more accurate.[3] The paper begins by assessing the extent of the institutional mortality problem in mid- and late-nineteenth-century London. Establishments for health care in this period of metropolitan history are placed into one of three broad categories: general and specialist voluntary hospitals; hospitals for infectious disease, including those administered by the Metropolitan Asylums Board (MAB); and workhouses and the infirmaries attached to them. Briefly outlining the ways in which the origin of deaths in workhouses and hospitals for infectious disease can be estimated, mortality in general and specialist voluntary hospitals is scrutinised in greater detail. Admission and death registers for a selection of these establishments are analysed and these sources allow the mortality catchment area of each hospital to be mapped. In a penultimate section, the automated procedure of redistributing the deaths to their original place of residence is described, after which the paper concludes with a selection of examples that demonstrate the potential impact of redistribution on the patterns and trends of epidemiological change in mid- and late-Victorian London.

The epidemiological problem

The number of people dying in metropolitan institutions in the second half of the nineteenth century can be calculated from the *Annual Reports of the Registrar-General.* Between 1851 and 1901, the proportion of all deaths in the capital that occurred in a hospital, a poor law establishment or a lunatic asylum rose from 15 to 40 per cent (Table 1). By the latter date, London was registering almost 30 per cent of national institutional deaths, but only 14 per cent of all mortality: the institutionalisation of death was more widely experienced in the metropolis than elsewhere. Yet within the capital, the level of institutional mortality of some districts greatly exceeded that of others. Thus, in 1861 no institutional deaths were registered in East London registration district, while only four per cent of the deaths in Lewisham and three per cent in St Luke's took place in an institution.[4] At the other extreme, the percentages in West London and St Olave, Southwark registration districts were 54 and 66 respectively. In heavily institutionalised localities such as these, the reported death rates were inflated by the presence of large hospitals (St Bartholomew's in West London and Guy's and St Thomas's in St Olave). By the same token, their residents dying in one of these hospitals may have artificially reduced the level of mortality in other districts.

	1851	1861	1871	1881	1891	1901
	%	%	%	%	%	%
Lunatic Asylums	0.7	0.4	0.4	0.4	0.5	0.5
Hospitals	5.7	6.4	9.3	9.8	10.4	13.8
Poor Law Institutions	8.9	8.8	8.3	10.7	13.7	16.6
Non-institutional	84.6	84.3	82.0	79.1	75.5	69.1
Total	100	100	100	100	100	100
N	55,488	65,251	80,430	81,346	89,122	78,224

Table 1. Deaths in London occurring in different types of institution, 1851–1901
Note: The percentage columns may not sum exactly to 100 because of rounding.
Source: Calculated from the relevant Annual Reports of the Registrar-General.

Not until 1911 did the Registrar-General use the information provided on death certificates to return the deaths of individuals to where they had lived.[5] Fortunately, one source of data reduces the magnitude of this problem. From 1885, and for a limited number of infectious diseases, the *Annual Summaries* of the *Weekly Returns* of the Registrar-General published tables of district mortality that redistributed the deaths occurring in institutions.[6] The period before this date remains troublesome. Until now, researchers have attempted to counteract the impact of institutional mortality by combining districts (and thus reducing the exchange of deaths between districts);[7] by eliminating from the analysis those districts where the degree of distortion brought about by the presence of institutions is considered excessively great;[8] or, for single causes of death, by 'returning' institutional deaths to their district of origin on a case-by-case basis.[9]

None of these approaches delivers a basic requirement of the epidemiological historian: a full dataset of metropolitan cause-specific mortality that is corrected for deaths in institutions.[10] To do this it is necessary to investigate the potential of source materials that were generated by the institutions themselves.

A solution can be successfully met only if it is recognised that each set of institutions presents a unique set of difficulties. Distinctions must be made between lunatic asylums, Poor Law establishments, and hospitals. The influence of the first can be disregarded since, as Table 1 showed, they rarely accounted for more than half of one per cent of deaths in London. Furthermore, because parish clerks seldom admitted to the workhouse paupers who lived in other parishes, a Poor Law institution only creates a serious distortion to the local mortality rate when a workhouse or workhouse infirmary was located beyond the boundary of the parish that administered it. Such establishments were termed 'outlying' workhouses. For example, in 1861, 119 deaths occurred in a workhouse that belonged to Strand but was located in Pancras. These 119 deaths were officially registered in Pancras and represented less than three per cent of the total Pancras mortality in that year. However, 119 deaths represent 12 per cent of Strand's 'official' mortality. In the event, only a small minority of individual registration districts were affected by the 'outlying' workhouse problem during the period 1860–1884.[11] In these 25 years, a total of 16,117 deaths have to be returned to their district of origin in this way, which represents an annual average of only 645 deaths.[12]

Far more intractable is the question of deaths in the hospitals of London, which possessed perhaps the densest network of institutional health provision of any city in the world at this time.[13] Accident and emergency cases were normally treated and admitted without question.[14] Otherwise, patient intake in the hospitals was thought to be highly filtered according to rules drawn up by the governing body of each hospital. Subscriptions from governors entitled them to letters of admission to in- and out-patient departments that secured treatment for family, friends, business associates and even employees.[15] However, it was not uncommon for hospitals to relax or even abandon these conditions.[16] Type of illness was also an important factor in determining the level mortality in a hospital. The regulations of almost every voluntary general hospital in London sought to exclude all cases of infectious disease and respiratory tuberculosis. Certainly, sufferers from such ailments were sometimes sent by the hospital on to either the parish workhouse or the London Fever Hospital in Islington.[17] Some hospitals even sought to develop specialities that ensured patients with a low mortality risk represented a large proportion of admissions: higher numbers discharged as 'cured' or 'relieved' as opposed to 'dead' were likely to bolster the reputation of an institution.[18] Unlike workhouses and their infirmaries, however, the general and specialist voluntary hospitals did not regulate admissions upon the basis of where the applicant lived. The potential catchment area of each hospital was unlimited.

Hospital registers

Readily available sources that enable us to map the residential origin of patients who died in hospital do not appear to exist on a systematic basis. Here, it is vital to delineate between the types of hospital under scrutiny, be it a general or specialist voluntary hospital, or one that admitted cases of infectious disease. We begin with the latter. For each disease that was treated, the annual *Reports* of the MAB hospitals regularly listed the districts from which patients were admitted.[19] But other than a total hospital mortality figure for each disease, these reports do not give additional geographical details regarding the usual place of residence of *dead* patients. For just 1868, 1869 and 1870, a similarly moderate level of information is provided by annual *Reports* of the London Fever Hospital in Islington. This was the main hospital in London for the treatment of fever patients before the MAB was created.[20] Reaching beyond the restricted limits of these published sources, the logical course of action in such instances would be to consult the original admission and discharge registers of the hospitals concerned. This is indeed possible for the London Fever Hospital. Consequently, cause of death and address of the 5,238 patients that died in the Hospital over the period 1860–75 have been extracted from the patient register. Comparable sources no longer exist for the MAB hospitals. The place of residence of deceased patients in these institutions must be estimated by using a complicated procedure that relies upon multiplying the case-fatality rate for each disease in each hospital by the number of admissions to the hospital from each metropolitan district.[21]

Clearly, it would be an extremely time-consuming task to extract from patient registers the place of origin for every person dying in the general and specialist voluntary hospitals between 1860–85. In 1860 alone there were over 3,200 deaths in such establishments.[22] The number of hospitals to be analysed therefore needs to be carefully controlled. For the purposes of redistributing mortality, an institution was considered sufficiently important for selection if in any year between 1860 and 1884 it contributed 10 per cent or more to the total mortality of the district in which it was situated. Ten hospitals that met these criteria are given in Table 2. Even though it did not comply with this 10 per cent rule, the Brompton Consumption Hospital was also included, since, in terms of mortality, it was by far the most important specialist hospital in the capital after the London Smallpox and Fever Hospitals in Islington.[23] On an annual basis, the eleven hospitals shown in Table 2 still accounted for about 3,000 deaths in London. Consequently, the dates studied were

Institution	Registration District	1861	1871	1881
Brompton Consumption Hospital	Kensington	127	128	110
St George's Hospital	St George Hanover Square	297	294	421
Westminster Hospital	Westminster†	143	151	168
Charing Cross Hospital	St Martin-in-the-Fields‡	70	142	139
Middlesex Hospital	Marylebone	235	246	327
King's College Hospital	Strand	147	184	180
Great Ormond Street Hospital For Sick Children	Holborn	99	79	105
St Bartholomew's Hospital	West London§	611	573	610
London Hospital	Whitechapel	366	550	665
Guy's Hospital (part)	St Saviour Southwark	22	10	–
Guy's Hospital (part)	St Olave Southwark	426	540	475
St Thomas's Hospital (part)*	St Saviour Southwark	93	121	444
St Thomas's Hospital (part)	St Olave Southwark	285	–	–
Total deaths		2,921	3,018	3,644

Table 2. Deaths in 11 London hospitals, 1861–81
Source: Relevant Annual Reports of the Registrar-General.

Notes:
† Incorporated into St George Hanover Square in 1870.
‡ Incorporated into Strand in 1868.
§ Incorporated into London City registration district in 1870.
* Deaths in St Thomas's Hospital were temporarily registered in Newington registration district between 1864 and 1869. Newington itself was incorporated into St Saviour Southwark in 1869 and from 1872 the hospital was located in Lambeth registration district.

limited to the census years 1861, 1871 and 1881. The task of compiling the database was further curtailed by the fact that relevant registers do not survive for St George's, the Westminster, King's College and Charing Cross Hospitals, while suitable material is available for the London Hospital only from 1883.

Adding the deaths extracted from the London Fever Hospital registers to all the deaths occurring in the relevant hospitals in the three years listed above gives a total of 11,216 deaths, each of which had to be allocated a district of origin. Of the 11,216 deaths, an address was not given in the registers for 103 of them. These deaths were excluded from the analysis. For many of the others, locating a registration district was a relatively straightforward undertaking, since it was not uncommon for the hospital clerk to record the district in which the patient normally lived. Although for a large minority of patients a more precise address was given—such as a street or road name—if this was not accompanied by the district in which the street was situated, then the address had to be linked to its district by consulting a diverse range of sources. These included census enumerators' street lists, London County Council architects' lists of London streets, Post Office directories and nineteenth-century maps of the capital.[24]

In practice, it was discovered that the hospital clerk usually recorded street names alone either if the street was very close to the hospital itself or if it was a long-established thoroughfare in the capital. Instances of the latter, such as Old Kent Road south of the River Thames or Caledonian Road in north London, were particularly problematic because they tended to cross the boundaries of two or more registration districts. The only realistic option was to allocate the deaths of people living on roads such as these to the district which contained the greatest proportion of the road's house numbers. Six hundred and eighty-eight different addresses were given in the registers consulted, including places beyond the metropolis. All but seven of them were allocated either to a registration district in London or to a residual 'outside London' category.[25] A Microsoft Access file containing three fields was created, one containing the 688 unique addresses, another relating to the registration district in which the address was located and a third providing the relevant registration subdistrict(s). This information was then used to assign automatically a registration district to the original address of each of the 11,216 hospital deaths.

Hospital catchment areas

From the Microsoft Access files, Excel spreadsheets were created of the metropolitan registration district catchment areas of each hospital for the three dates that were examined. Saved as Comma Separated files, these spreadsheets were then transferred into an Arc/Info Geographic Information System (GIS) containing digitised boundary files for the registration districts and subdistricts in London from 1840 to 1920.[26] Coverages of the registration district boundaries for 1861, 1871 and 1881 were used to map the mortality catchment areas of the seven hospitals.[27] The greatest number of hospital deaths in the institutions chosen for analysis occurred in 1881 and maps for that year (1883 for the London Hospital) are shown in Figures 1 to 7.[28] (A map of the registration districts in 1881 can be found in the Appendix.)

It appears that the majority of patients who died in the general voluntary hospitals were drawn from areas very close to the hospital itself. At St Bartholomew's, for example, 12 per cent came from London City (the district where the hospital was located, see Table 2) and more than 24 per cent from adjoining Holborn (Figure 1). A further nine per cent originated in Hackney, and between four and eight per cent from Islington, Shoreditch and Bethnal Green. The Great Ormond Street Hospital for Sick Children was little more than half a mile from St Bartholomew's, and it too admitted from Holborn (12.5) and Islington (13.5) many of the patients who eventually died there, as well as nearly one quarter (24.0) from Pancras (Figure 2). In 1883, the London Hospital in Whitechapel appears to have been a magnet for terminally ill patients in the east end (Figure 3). With 15.1 per cent, the most significant district of origin within London was Whitechapel itself, but neighbouring east end districts of Poplar (11.8), Stepney (11.0), Bethnal Green (10.1), Mile End Old Town (9.0), Shoreditch (1.6) and St George in the East (12.5) together contributed an additional 56 per cent. Turning westwards, the Middlesex Hospital's mortality catchment area in 1881 was even more dramatically concentrated upon just two districts (Figure 4). A little over 65 per cent of the patients dying there had lived either in Marylebone (44.6) or in Pancras (20.6). It is significant that no district south of the River Thames contributed as much as three per cent to any of these hospitals' mortality in 1881, perhaps because patients from south London heavily relied on the services provided by

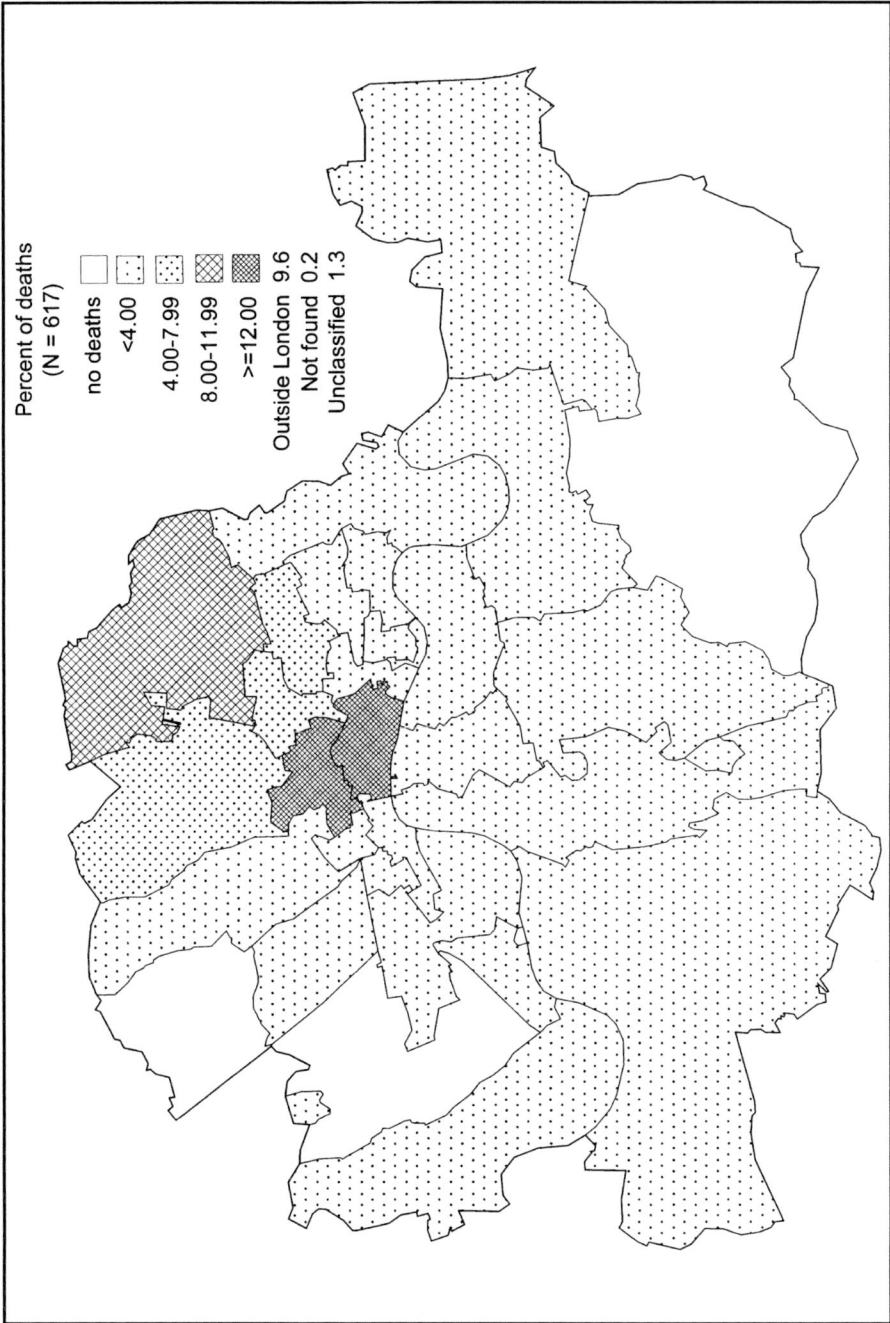

Percent of deaths (N = 617)

☐	no deaths
⠌	<4.00
⠷	4.00-7.99
▨	8.00-11.99
▩	>=12.00

Outside London 9.6
Not found 0.2
Unclassified 1.3

Figure 1. Mortality catchment area, St Bartholomew's Hospital, 1881

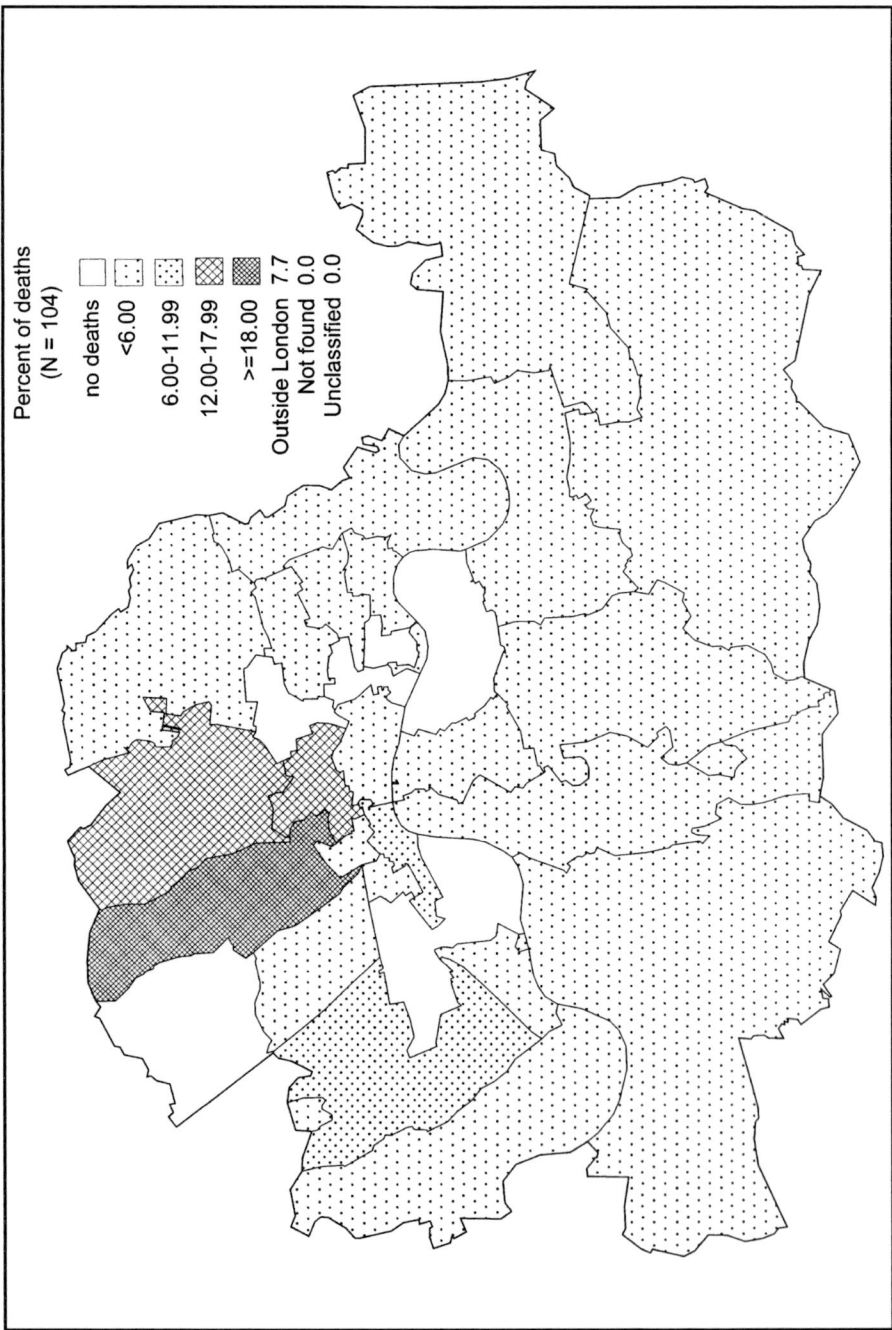

Percent of deaths (N = 104)

no deaths	
<6.00	
6.00–11.99	
12.00–17.99	
>=18.00	

Outside London	7.7
Not found	0.0
Unclassified	0.0

Figure 2. Mortality catchment area, Great Ormond Street Hospital for Sick Children, 1881

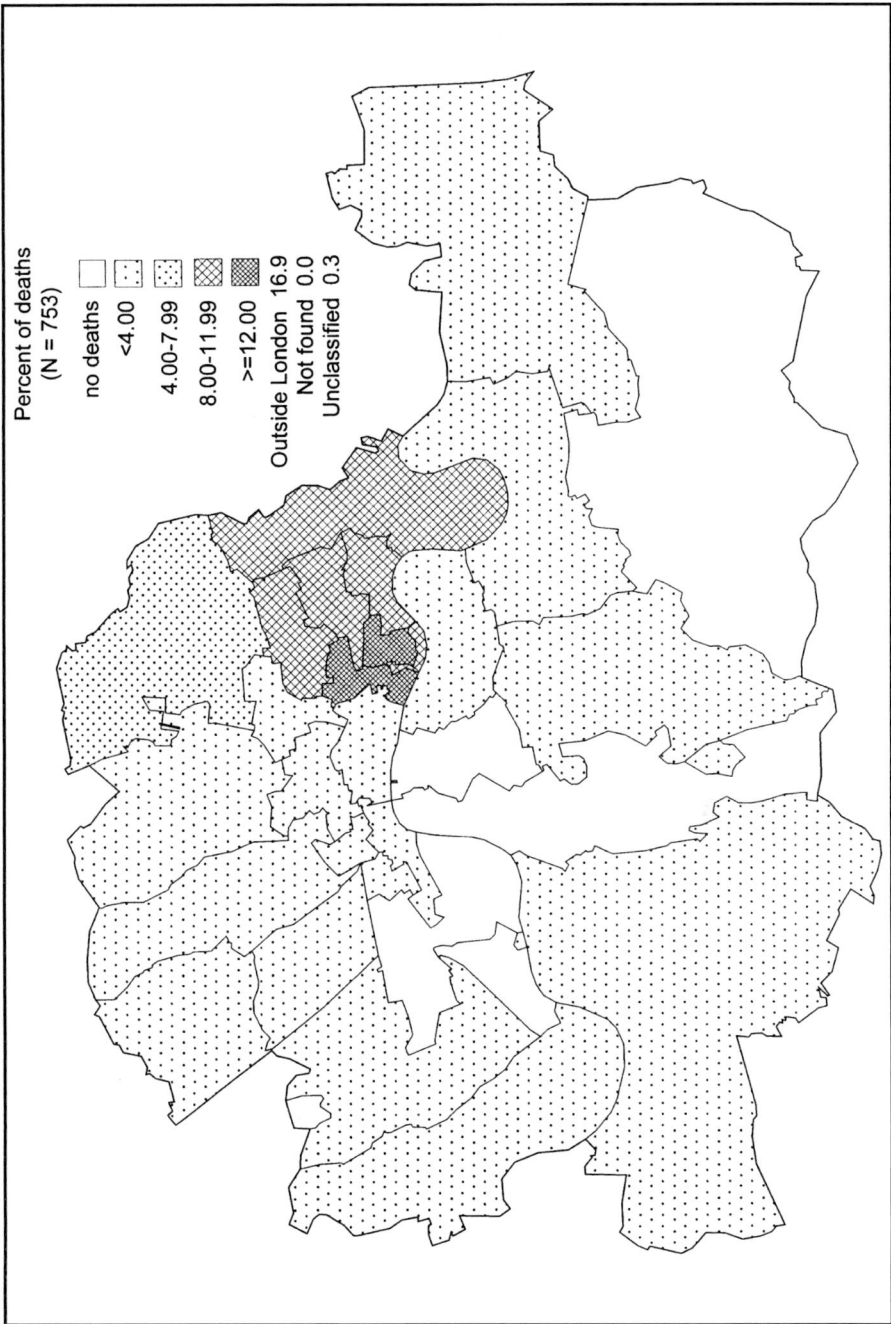

Figure 3. Mortality catchment area, The London Hospital, 1883

Percent of deaths
(N = 753)

no deaths

<4.00

4.00-7.99

8.00-11.99

>=12.00

Outside London 16.9
Not found 0.0
Unclassified 0.3

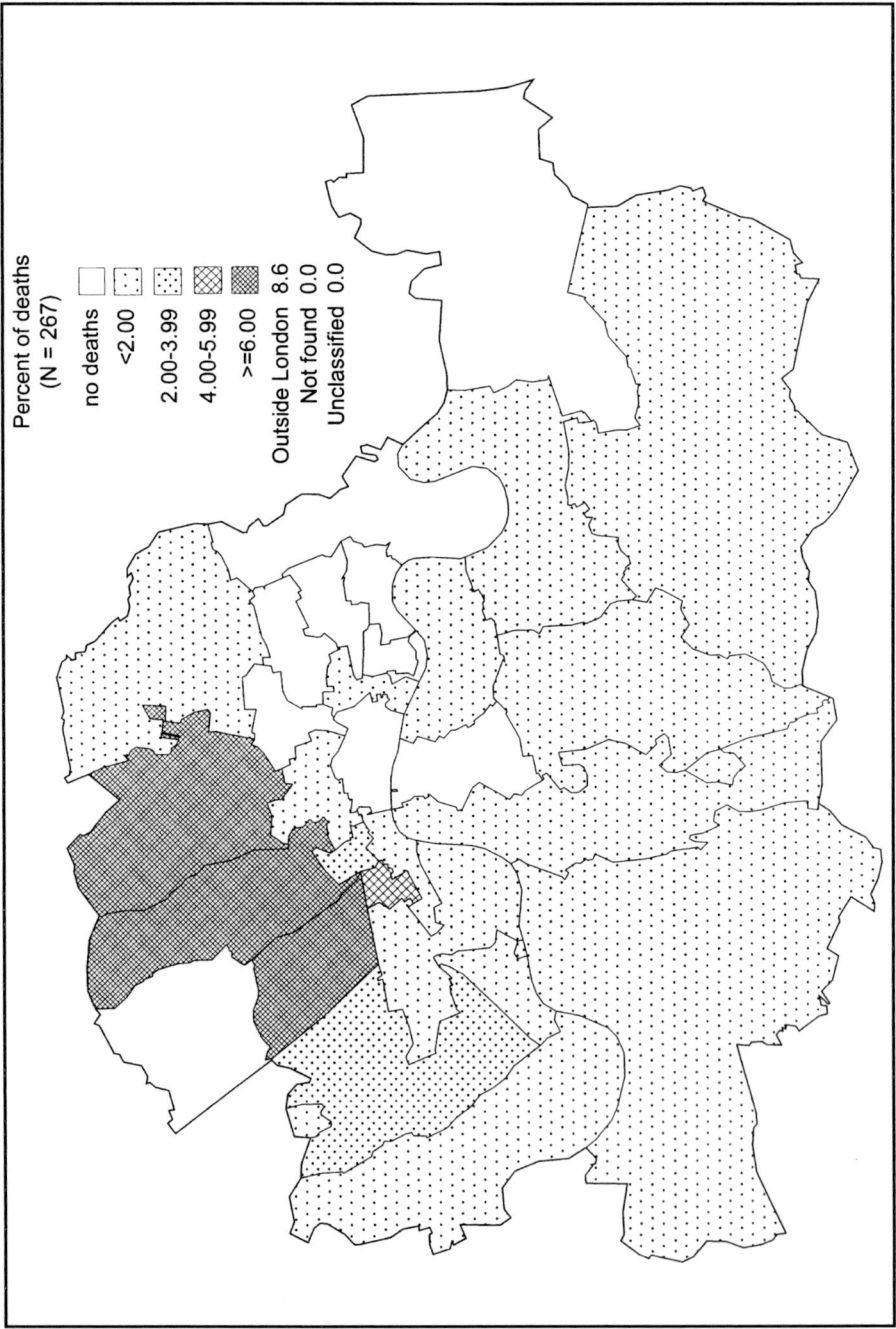

Percent of deaths
(N = 267)

no deaths
<2.00
2.00-3.99
4.00-5.99
>=6.00

Outside London 8.6
Not found 0.0
Unclassified 0.0

Figure 4. Mortality catchment area, Middlesex Hospital, 1881

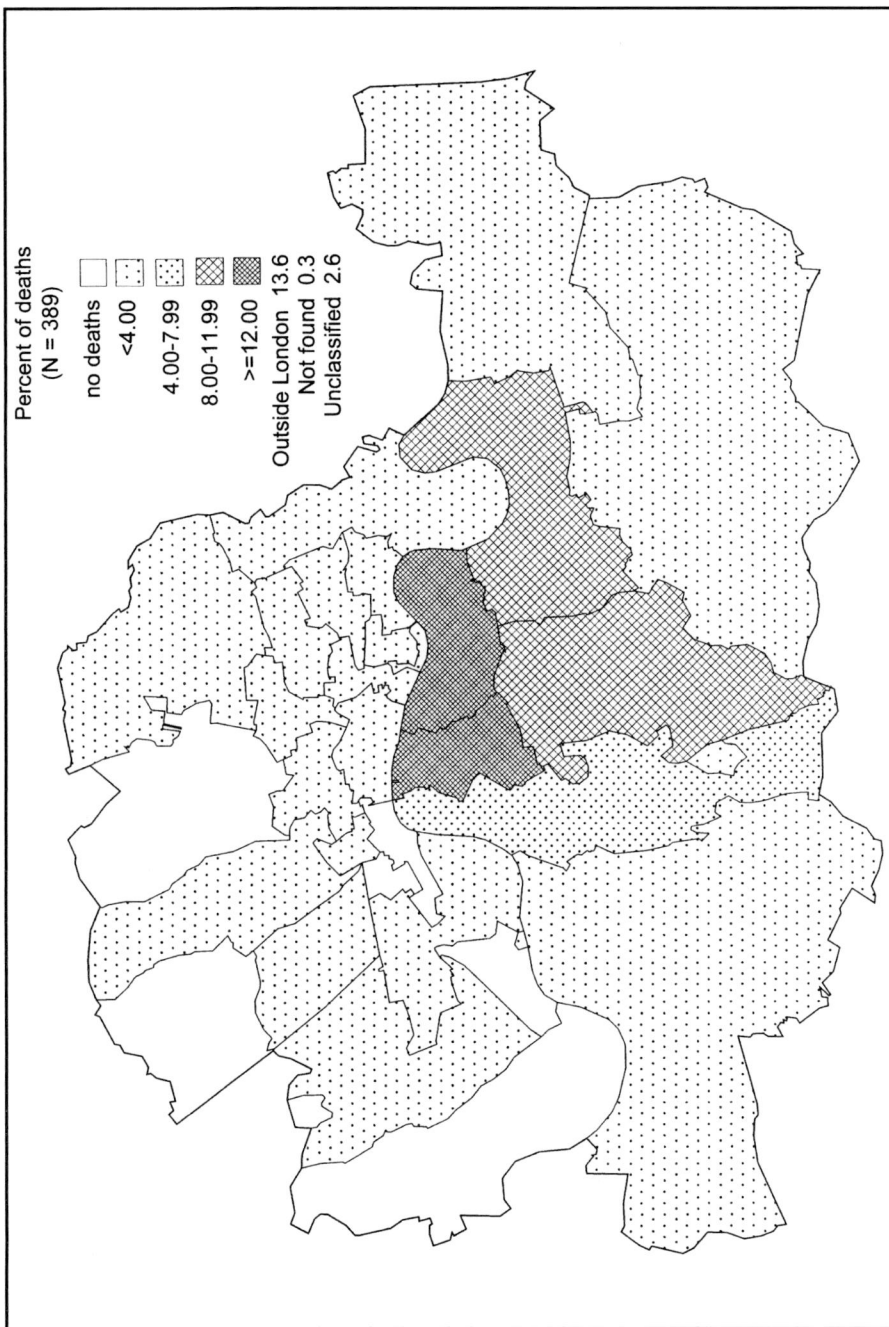

Percent of deaths
(N = 389)

no deaths	
<4.00	
4.00-7.99	
8.00-11.99	
>=12.00	
Outside London	13.6
Not found	0.3
Unclassified	2.6

Figure 5. Mortality catchment area, Guy's Hospital, 1881

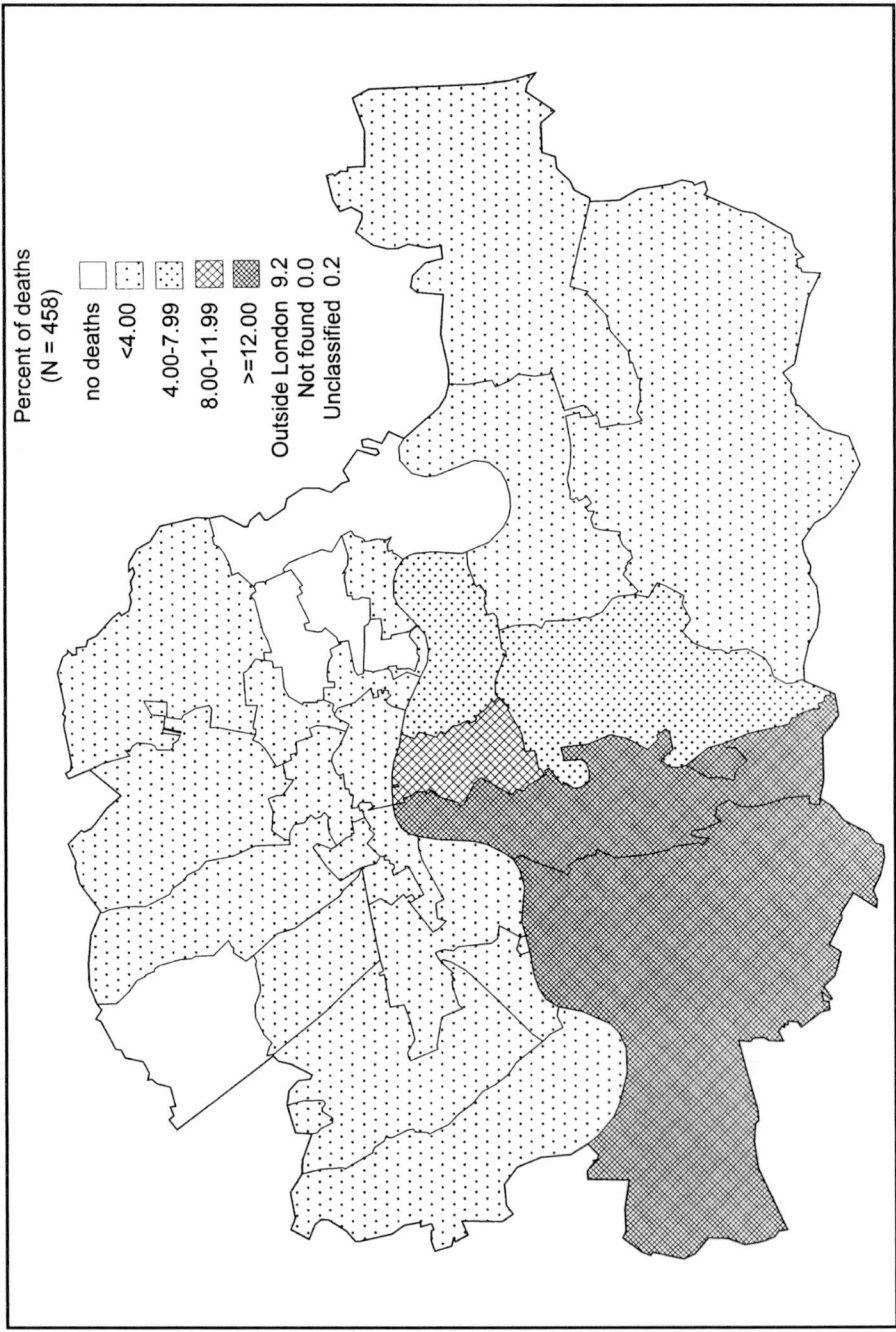

Percent of deaths (N = 458)

no deaths	
<4.00	
4.00-7.99	
8.00-11.99	
>=12.00	

Outside London 9.2
Not found 0.0
Unclassified 0.2

Figure 6. Mortality catchment area, St Thomas's Hospital, 1881

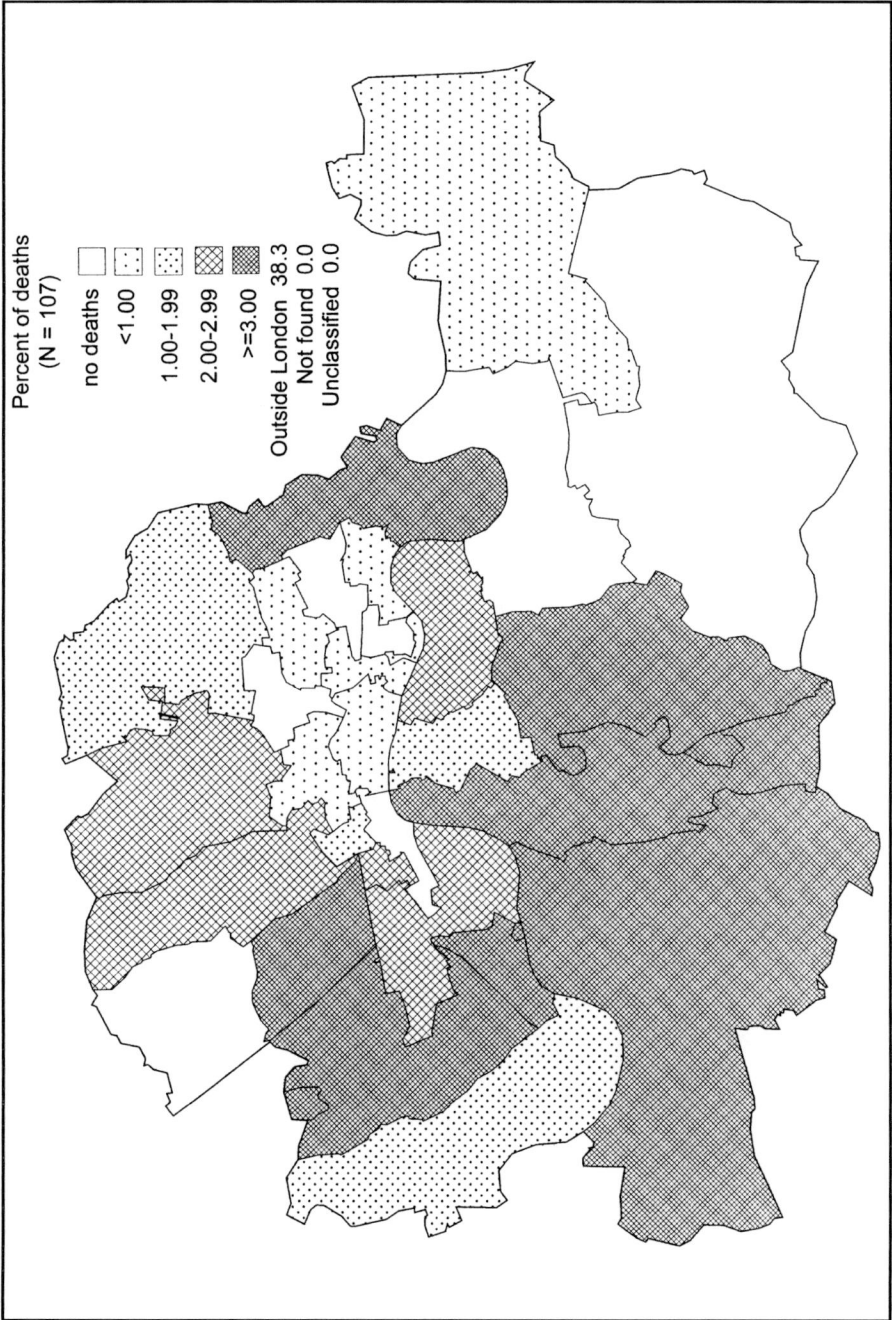

Percent of deaths
(N = 107)

no deaths

<1.00

1.00-1.99

2.00-2.99

>=3.00

Outside London 38.3
Not found 0.0
Unclassified 0.0

Figure 7. Mortality catchment area, Brompton Consumption Hospital, 1881

Guy's and St Thomas's Hospitals. In the case of the former, more than 40 per cent of dead patients came from the two Southwark districts, St Saviour (17.7) and St Olave (23.1) (Figure 5). Lambeth patients accounted for 38.4 per cent of deaths in St Thomas's Hospital, with a further 6.1 per cent having lived in Camberwell and 14.4 per cent in Wandsworth (Figure 6). In a mirror image of the other voluntary general hospitals in the analysis, very few patients who died had crossed the river from north London to be admitted to Guy's and St Thomas's in the south.

Although it has already been noted that possession of a subscriber's letter was normally an essential pre-condition of access to treatment in a hospital for anything other than an emergency case, the maps of mortality catchment areas suggest that the close residential proximity of many patients admitted to each hospital was also significant. This is not to dismiss the fact that many patients in any given hospital did indeed live in parts of the metropolis that were not very close to the hospital. Thus, in 1881, more than 38 per cent of the total deaths occurring in the hospitals shown in Figures 1 to 6 came from areas that lay within the boundary of the metropolis but outside the sector in which the institution was located. For instance, 61 per cent of St Bartholomew's deaths originated beyond the limits of central London as defined by the Registrar-General (see Appendix). Of course, the validity of such examples depends upon the population size and boundary of each district group. But one quarter of the deaths in St Thomas's were from metropolitan districts outside south London, even though this district group had a population exceeding 960,000 in 1881. It is likely that the wide dispersal of deaths beyond the immediate locale of a hospital reflects the facts that those subscribers who were rewarded with letters did not necessarily live close to the hospital itself, that the rules for admission were frequently abandoned, or that there was an increasing degree of specialization that attracted patients from greater distances.[29]

While the large hospitals were eager to advertise the compassionate work they carried out for the poor citizens of the metropolis, claims were also made that their outstanding reputations caused many patients to travel from far and wide to seek treatment and cure from their distinguished staff.[30] Rarely was evidence ever brought forward to substantiate these claims.[31] But it was true at least for a specialist institution such as the Brompton Consumption Hospital. Many of the patients (38.3 per cent) ending their days in this hospital in 1881 lived not only outside Kensington, but also outside London (Figure 7).[32] For most of the hospitals discussed, however, the registers show that only ten per cent of dead patients habitually came from beyond the metropolitan limits.[33] This is not a trivial proportion; and it refers only to dead patients rather than all in- and outpatients. Nevertheless, it suggests that re-evaluation of some hospitals' propagandist assertions is required if we are to achieve a more nuanced understanding of how the metropolitan health system operated.

Redistributing mortality

Although each death that occurred in the voluntary hospitals that have been studied may now be returned to the metropolitan district in which the patient usually lived, additional complications must be considered. First, the data was collected for only three years, 1861, 1871 and 1881. The geographical patterns that have been shown for 1881 were in fact very closely matched by the other years. Consequently, the residential origin of dead patients in the intervening periods (as well as 1860 and 1882–84) may be estimated with a certain degree of confidence.

Second, the evidence provided by the hospital registers that still exist can be used to estimate the pattern of residence of dead patients in those hospitals where the relevant sources no longer remain. More precisely, deaths in Charing Cross, King's College, St George's and Westminster Hospitals can be redistributed at the three broad levels identified earlier. First, a fixed proportion was given over to the 'outside London' category, according to the average percentage of such deaths occurring in the hospitals for which the data can be collected. A further percentage was allocated to each district beyond the sector of London in which the hospital was situated, distributed according to the population of each district.[34] Finally, the remaining percentage of deaths were divided between the districts of the sector in which the hospital was located, also in proportion to the population living in each district in that sector.[35] To take a specific example, of the 168 deaths occurring in Westminster Hospital in 1881, 22 (13 per cent) were allocated to the residual 'outside London' category. Thirty-four dead patients (20 percent) were estimated to have lived in St. George Hanover Square, the district in which the Hospital was sited at that date. A total of 69 deaths (41 per cent) were distributed between the other registration districts in the West London sector, namely Kensington, Fulham, Chelsea and Westminster. The remaining 43 deaths were allocated to all the London districts beyond this sector. Needless to say, many changes in the composition and boundaries of metropolitan registration districts took place between 1861 and 1884. Institutional deaths therefore were allocated according to the district boundaries that were in existence in each year.

Finally, cause of death must be dealt with. Along with much other useful information regarding the patient and his/her stay in hospital, the patient registers frequently supplied the cause of death. However, cause of death was not transcribed because it was feared that the three benchmark years (or any others) would fail to provide an accurate portrayal of the diseases that were seen in individual general voluntary hospitals in other years.[36] It was considered that fewer problems would arise by applying the cause of death structure recorded for all the metropolitan general hospitals by the Registrar-General in 1861 to the deaths in each hospital for the period 1860–84.[37] Significant adjustments to this procedure were made for respiratory tuberculosis, other respiratory diseases, violent deaths and cholera in 1866. Thus, each death that was returned to a metropolitan district from a general voluntary hospital had a cause associated to it.

The redistribution procedure was carried out by performing two calculations on two sets of data that were held as tables in Microsoft Access. The first set, File A, contained the original tables of deaths by cause published by the Registrar-General for the metropolitan registration districts during the period 1860–84.[38] The second set of data, File B, comprised the number of deaths in each of the hospitals and 'outlying' workhouses. These were disaggregated by district of origin and by cause of death. The deaths in File B were first subtracted from the district in which each hospital was situated. For example, the annual deaths in the Middlesex Hospital were removed from the deaths in File A that were recorded in Marylebone, those in Great Ormond Street Hospital were taken from Holborn and so on. The second step simply involved returning the institutional deaths to the metropolitan district from whence they came.

Epidemiological impact

The results of the analysis of hospital mortality catchment areas not only represent a step forward in our knowledge of medical care in mid- and late-Victorian London. They also play an important role in rewriting the capital's epidemiological history during this period. Having described how deaths in the general and specialist hospitals have been redistributed, it is now possible to illustrate the impact of the method on interpretation of patterns of crude death rates in the metropolis.[39] We begin with 1881, the year for which the hospital mortality catchment areas have already been drawn. Table 3 contains the district crude death rates calculated from the original tables published in the Registrar-General's *Annual Report* as well as the rates that have been corrected according to the methods outlined in this paper. Initially, we might note that redistribution reduces the amount of variation across the metropolis: at 3.50, the standard deviation of the corrected crude death rates is lower than that of 4.09 for the uncorrected ones.[40] The rank order of the districts for each set of rates is listed in bold type. After redistribution only four districts—Fulham, Hampstead, Mile End Old Town and Lewisham—retained their relative position. Another set of districts—such as Kensington, Marylebone, Pancras, Whitechapel and Wandsworth—changed their standing only slightly. A further tier—St George Hanover Square, Shoreditch, St Olave Southwark, for example—moved by five or six places. In contrast, the status of three places shifted considerably. Out of 29 districts in all, Stepney fell from 16th to 25th position and Holborn from 9th to 24th. Undoubtedly, these districts were net 'exporters' of deaths to institutions in surrounding areas and the return of these deaths served to increase their level of mortality. The opposite was the case in Strand, which jumped from being the fourth worst district in London to the seventh best. Here, removing the great majority of deaths in Charing Cross and King's College Hospitals reduced the crude death rate from 27.16 to 19.09 per 1,000.[41] These extreme examples aside, comparing the rank order alone does not reveal the full extent of some changes. For instance, Whitechapel, as noted above, improved its position by only one place. Yet redistribution of the deaths in the London Hospital in 1881 had in fact reduced the crude death rate from above 33 per thousand to below 27.

Perhaps an even better idea can be gained of how the level of mortality may change after redistribution by plotting corrected and uncorrected rates through time. Figure 8 does this between 1860 and 1890 for two contrasting districts, Whitechapel and Holborn. We have seen how the crude death rate of the latter in 1881 was raised by about three points per 1,000 after correcting for institutional mortality (Table 3). This increase was replicated throughout the period under review. Alternatively, Whitechapel's mortality rate was greatly reduced, dropping by as much as nine points per 1,000 in 1887. The striking feature of Figure 8 is the way in which two districts with apparently divergent records of mortality were in fact far more closely related, in terms of health status, than was previously imagined.

	Uncorrected		Corrected	
	Rank	CDR	Rank	CDR
Kensington	4	17.34	3	17.35
Fulham	15	21.53	15	21.80
Chelsea	18	22.08	20	23.08
St. George Hanover Sq	10	20.85	4	17.71
Westminster	8	20.00	14	21.67
Marylebone	14	21.47	13	21.43
Hampstead	1	13.62	1	13.79
Pancras	19	22.12	18	22.84
Islington	7	19.86	9	19.89
Hackney	13	21.40	11	20.81
St. Giles	20	22.45	23	23.81
Strand	26	27.16	7	19.09
Holborn	9	20.46	24	23.96
London City	28	28.56	26	24.73
Shoreditch	22	23.71	16	22.33
Bethnal Green	23	24.13	27	25.41
Whitechapel	29	33.08	28	26.94
St. George-in-the-East	27	28.27	29	31.00
Stepney	16	21.85	25	24.23
Mile End Old Town	12	21.38	12	21.18
Poplar	21	22.52	17	22.43
St. Saviour Southwark	17	21.88	21	23.38
St. Olave Southwark	24	24.85	19	22.93
Lambeth	11	21.31	8	19.62
Wandsworth	5	17.39	6	18.24
Camberwell	6	18.71	10	20.02
Greenwich	25	26.35	22	23.75
Lewisham	2	14.33	2	14.75
Woolwich	3	17.33	5	17.93
Standard deviation		4.09		3.50

Table 3 Uncorrected and corrected crude death rates (per 1,000 population), London registration districts, 1881
Source: Uncorrected rates calculated from 44th Annual Report of the Registrar-General, 1881.

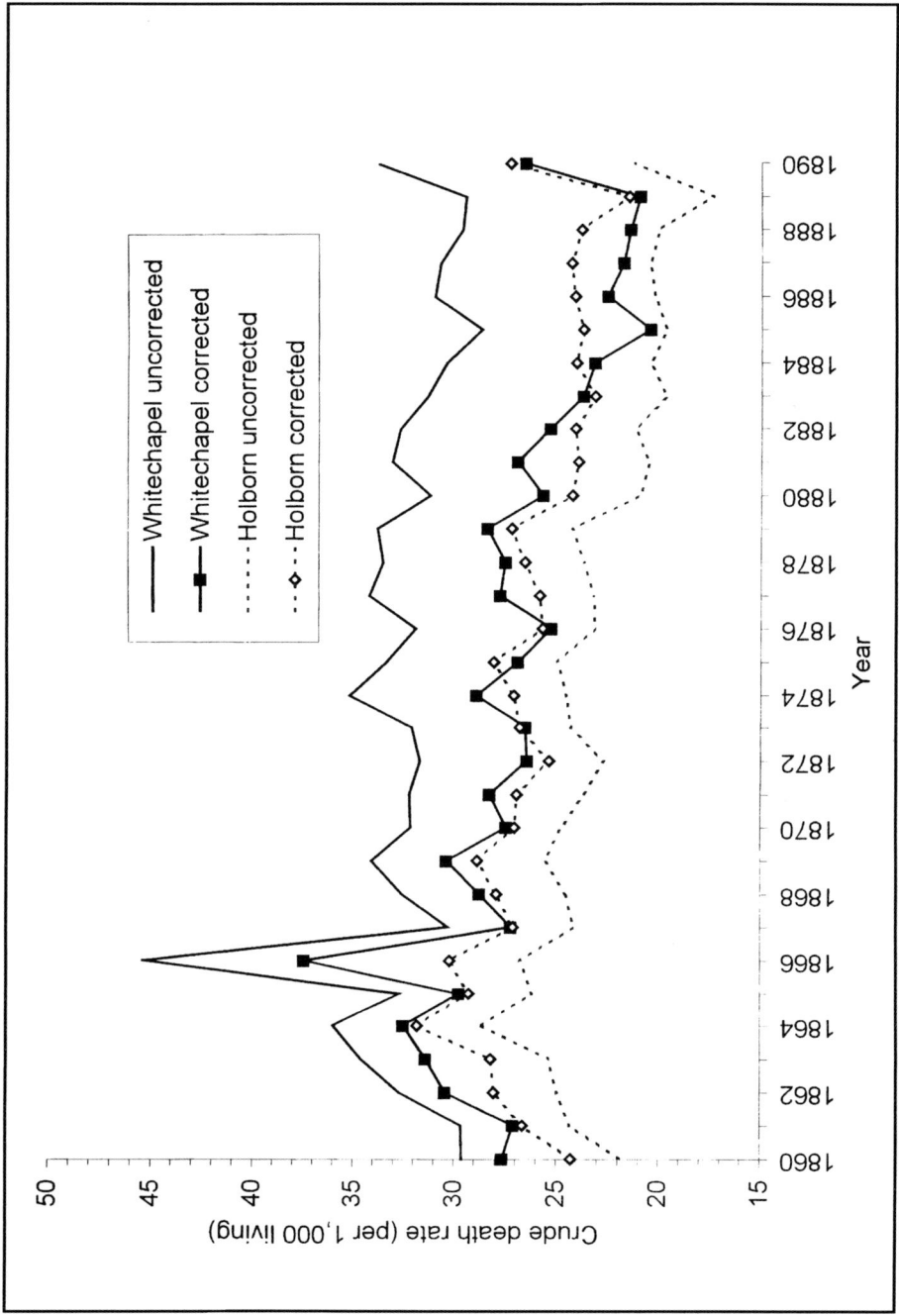

Figure 8. Corrected and uncorrected crude death rates, Holborn and Whitechapel, 1860–90

Discussion and Conclusion

In order to produce a more accurate and representative dataset of district mortality in London in the second half of the nineteenth century, this paper has sought to describe the methods by which deaths in the various institutions of London were returned to their normal place of origin during the acutely problematic period 1860–84. Alternative methods of redistribution were developed for each type of institution. On the one hand, returning deaths occurring in workhouses and workhouse infirmaries proved to be relatively straightforward. On the other, the lack of suitable archival material for infectious disease hospitals raised a complex set of obstacles. In the case of the MAB establishments, an indirect method of estimating the origin of deaths by using hospital case fatality rates had to be employed. It proved necessary to consult patient registers for the London Fever Hospital. A similar approach was adopted for a range of general and specialist voluntary hospitals and mortality catchment areas of these important institutions have been examined in detail.

It must be admitted that the source materials and methods of redistribution are not without their weaknesses. One cannot be sure, for example, that the usual place of residence was truthfully provided by every patient or transcribed accurately by the admissions clerk. Evaluating the causes of death in the hospitals provided by the 1861 *Annual Report of the Registrar-General* is also problematic, partly because a person may have contracted a disease during their period as an in-patient and partly because the structure of hospital mortality may have changed over time. In addition, it may be unsafe to use the mortality catchment areas of some hospitals to reconstruct those of others where the required source materials no longer exist.

These and other reservations may be countered by the argument that a wide range of sources have been consulted to ensure that the results were indeed representative of the broad experience of institutional mortality across the metropolis. Ultimately, however, it is the comparison of uncorrected with corrected crude death rates that demonstrates the strengths of the redistribution procedure. Firstly, the rates for each district were adjusted in a direction, up or down, that common sense and historical knowledge suggested they ought to be. Secondly, the rates corrected in the early 1880s corresponded very closely to those calculated from the redistributed mortality tables that appeared from 1885 in the Registrar-General's *Annual Summaries* of the *Weekly Returns.* As a result of these strategies and reconstructions, the more accurate annual levels of mortality that have been produced now allow the geography of metropolitan mortality decline and epidemiology in the period 1860–1920 to be interpreted with confidence.

Acknowledgements

The research for this chapter forms part of a project 'Mortality in the Metropolis, 1860–1920', based at the Centre for Metropolitan History and generously funded by the Wellcome Trust. Bill Luckin (the project co-ordinator) and Andrea Tanner collected data from the hospital registers and helped to formulate the questions, analysis and conclusions that appear here. Comments and advice from Derek Keene, Bob Woods and various seminar audiences have been gratefully received. Humphrey Southall and Ian Gregory from the Department of Geography, University of Portsmouth, created the GIS. Ian Gregory provided a great deal of practical assistance with the production of the maps. Archivists at the relevant hospitals and at the London Metropolitan Archive greatly facilitated the research.

Appendix

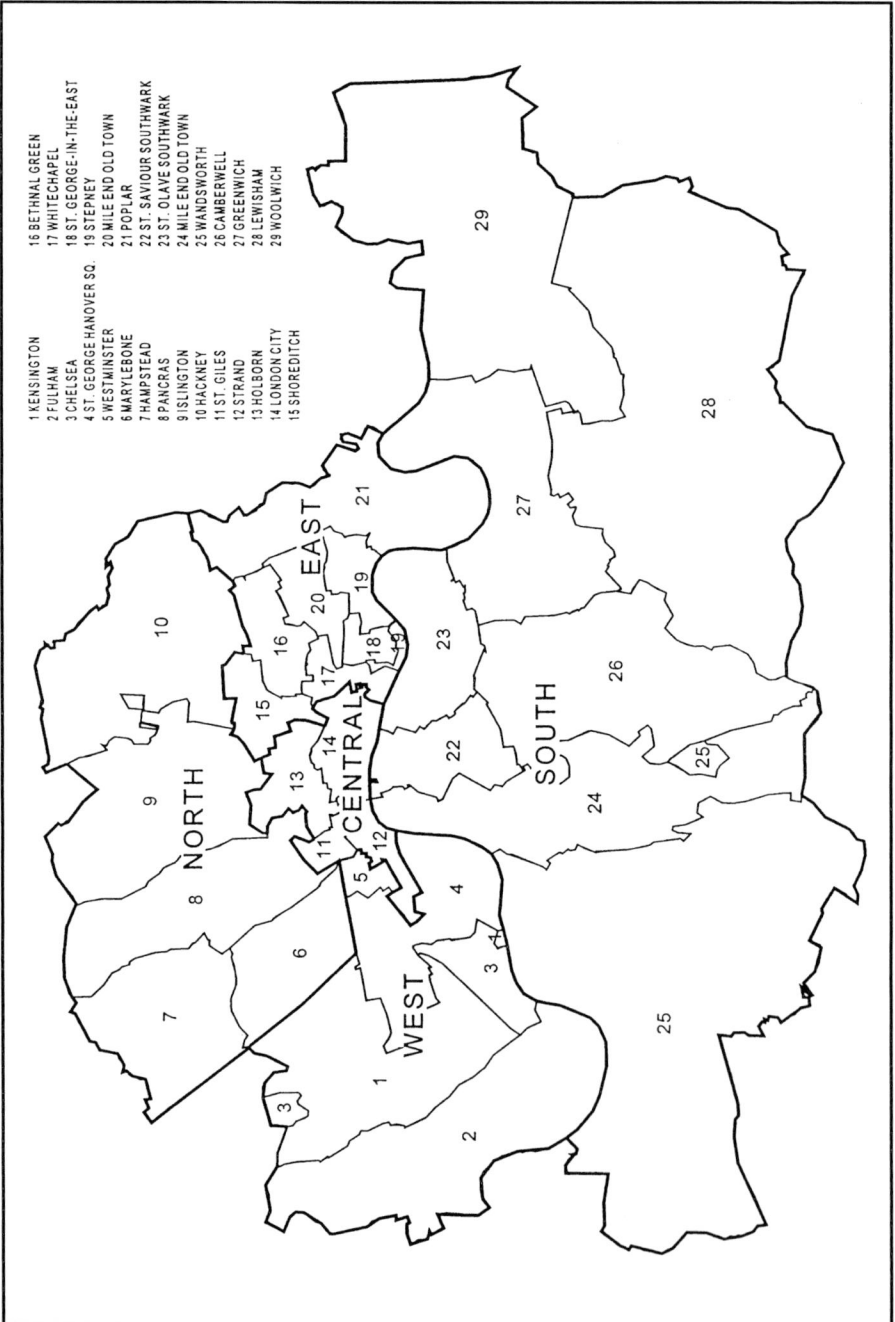

Figure 9. Map of London registration districts, 1881

The map legend lists the following districts:

1 KENSINGTON
2 FULHAM
3 CHELSEA
4 ST. GEORGE HANOVER SQ.
5 WESTMINSTER
6 MARYLEBONE
7 HAMPSTEAD
8 PANCRAS
9 ISLINGTON
10 HACKNEY
11 ST. GILES
12 STRAND
13 HOLBORN
14 LONDON CITY
15 SHOREDITCH
16 BETHNAL GREEN
17 WHITECHAPEL
18 ST. GEORGE-IN-THE-EAST
19 STEPNEY
20 MILE END OLD TOWN
21 POPLAR
22 ST. SAVIOUR SOUTHWARK
23 ST. OLAVE SOUTHWARK
24 MILE END OLD TOWN
25 WANDSWORTH
26 CAMBERWELL
27 GREENWICH
28 LEWISHAM
29 WOOLWICH

NOTES

[1] See W. Luckin, 'Death and survival in the city: approaches to the history of disease', *Urban History Yearbook* (1980), 53-61; A. Hardy, '"Death is the cure of all diseases": using the General Register Office cause of death statistics for 1837-1920', *Social History of Medicine,* 7 (1994), 472-92; R. I. Woods and N. Shelton, *An atlas of Victorian mortality* (Liverpool, 1997).

[2] See J. Riley, *Sick not dead. The health of British workingmen during the mortality decline* (Baltimore, 1997).

[3] A much longer paper than this one describes in greater depth the methodologies used for institutional mortality redistribution, G. Mooney, W. Luckin and A. Tanner, 'Patient pathways: solving the problem of institutional mortality in London in the later nineteenth century', *Social History of Medicine,* 12 (1999), 227-69. Whilst some overlap between that paper and this chapter is unavoidable, information is provided here on the computing techniques employed, a more detailed account (via maps) of the origins of patients dying in individual hospitals is given, and additional examples of how mortality rates are affected by institutionalisation are presented.

[4] In 1870 East London was merged with West London and London City to form the London City registration district that appears on the Appendix map. Similarly, St Luke's joined Clerkenwell and Holborn in 1869 to form a new Holborn registration district.

[5] See E. Higgs, 'The statistical Big Bang of 1911: ideology, technical innovation and the production of medical statistics', *Social History of Medicine,* 9 (1996), 409-26.

[6] From 1882 local registrars of births, deaths and marriages supplied each metropolitan Medical Officer of Health with a weekly list of deaths to individuals in institutions and the districts in which they had lived. See G. Mooney, 'Professionalization in public health and the measurement of sanitary progress in nineteenth century England and Wales', *Social History of Medicine,* 10 (1997), 53-78.

[7] G. Mooney, 'Did London pass the "sanitary test"? Seasonal infant mortality in London, 1870-1914', *Journal of Historical Geography,* 20 (1994), 158-74.

[8] N. Williams and G. Mooney, 'Infant mortality in an "age of great cities": London and the provincial cities compared, c. 1840-1910', *Continuity and Change,* 9 (1994), 195-96.

[9] W. Luckin, 'Evaluating the sanitary revolution: typhus and typhoid in London, 1851-1900', in R.I. Woods and J.H. Woodward, eds, *Urban disease and mortality in nineteenth century England* (London, 1984), 102-19.

[10] Basic outlines of the institutional problem in London can be found in Luckin, 'Death and survival' and A. Hardy, *The Epidemic Streets: Infectious Disease and the Rise of Preventive Medicine 1856-1900* (Oxford, 1993), Appendix, 297-301.

[11] W. Luckin and G. Mooney, 'Urban history and historical epidemiology: the case of London, 1860-1920', *Urban History,* 24 (1997), 37-55.

[12] A discussion of the way in which the patterns of age at death and cause of death in workhouses differ from those in the general population can be found in Mooney, Luckin and Tanner, 'Patient pathways', 241-45.

[13]   For a general treatment, see G. Rivett, *The Development of the London Hospital System, 1832-1982* (London, 1986).

[14]   According to the hospital authorities, Charing Cross Hospital treated about 7,400 accident and emergency cases annually. The fact that so many victims of street accidents were seen in the casualty department was used to advertise to students the advantages of studying medicine at the Hospital. See Charing Cross Hospital and School of Medicine, *Annual Report 1884-85,* 6.

[15]   On the abuse of the hospital system, see K. Waddington, 'Unsuitable cases: the debate over outpatient admissions, the medical profession and late-Victorian London Hospitals', *Medical History,* 42 (1998), 26-46; and *Charity and the London Hospitals, 1850-98* (Suffolk, 2000), 87-95.

[16]   In 1868 one hospital made admission to its outpatient department completely free of charge, enabling it 'to exercise much more control over the admission of patients than when they brought governors' letters, when it was difficult under such circumstances to refuse any', St George's Hospital, *Annual Report, 1875,* 4. Between 1840 and 1855, King's College Hospital admitted to its wards 6,107 people in possession of a subscriber's letter, a total that was dwarfed by the 13,069 admitted without one. King's College Hospital, *Report for 1856* (London, 1857), 19.

[17]   Guy's and other general hospitals arranged to send contagious cases northwards to the London Fever Hospital, Guy's Hospital, *Annual Report, 1876,* 435-36. This position was confirmed by evidence of St Bartholomew's witness recorded in the *House of Lords Select Committee on Metropolitan Hospitals, Second Report,* PP 1890-91, XIII, 827.

[18]   In a deliberate attempt to reduce its mortality rate, Guy's Hospital treated many more eye patients in the 1860s and 1870s than it had previously. See Mooney, Luckin and Tanner, 'Patient pathways', 235.

[19]   These *Reports* are held at the London Metropolitan Archive. On the history of the MAB, see G. Ayers, *England's first state hospitals: the Metropolitan Asylums Board* (London, 1971).

[20]   The London Smallpox Hospital, also in Islington, admitted many sufferers of the disease during the great epidemic of 1871-2. Patient registers are available only from 1878, so with the exception of 1871-72, the residential origin of deaths before this year must be estimated. Official reports by the Medical Officers of the Privy Council enable the redistribution of the Hospital's smallpox deaths in 1871-2, see E. Seaton, 'Report on the late epidemic of smallpox in the United Kingdom in its relation to vaccination and the vaccination laws', in *Annual Report of the Medical Officer of the Privy Council and the Local Government Board, 1874,* New Series IV, PP 1875, XL.

[21]   More detail of this procedure can be found in Mooney, Luckin and Tanner, 'Patient pathways', 253-59.

[22]   Calculations made from the *23rd Annual Report of the Registrar General, 1860* (London, 1862), 82-3 show that in London there were 3,039 deaths in 15 general hospitals and in 215 deaths in hospitals for special diseases (not including the London Fever and London Smallpox Hospitals).

23 For example: 159 deaths in the Brompton Consumption Hospital in 1860 compared to 16 in the Cancer Hospital, also in Brompton; and 34 deaths in the City of London Hospital for Diseases of the Chest, located in Bethnal Green.

24 Maps consulted include Edward Stanford's *1862 Library map of London and its suburbs* (London, 1980) and Bacon's 1888 *New large-scale ordnance atlas of London & Suburbs,* reproduced in Guildhall Library, *The A to Z of Victorian London* (London, 1987).

25 The amalgamation or splitting of registration districts, or the transference of a small area between two districts, means that in different years the same address might belong to a different district. For example, Northampton Square in Goswell Street subdistrict was situated in Clerkenwell until Holborn absorbed that registration district in 1869.

26 The London GIS was developed as part of the Great Britain Historical Database at the Department of Geography, University of Portsmouth. See Great Britain Historical Database Online, http://www.geog.port.ac.uk/gbhgis/ [6 September 2000].

27 The GIS allows the maps to be saved in PostScript or Illustrator format. The latter was used here to finalise the presentation of the maps for publication.

28 In no instance did the number of deaths extracted from the hospital register tally with that enumerated in the *Annual Reports of the Registrar-General* (see Table 2). The discrepancies ranged from one death in the case of Great Ormond Street Hospital to a shortfall of 60 deaths for the Middlesex Hospital. The reasons for such differences are not known, but the representativeness of the data extracted from the registers is unlikely to be undermined.

29 King's College Hospital, *Report for 1856,* 21-64 gives a list of governors and subscribers with their addresses.

30 Such testimonies were usually made when appeals for funding were underway. See King's College Hospital, *Report for 1856,* 5.

31 Although see the inpatient catchment area for St Thomas's in 1861 reproduced by Rivett, *The London Hospital System,* 98, and that for in- and outpatients at King's College Hospital for the period 1840-56, *Report, 1856,* 18.

32 It is not inconceivable that many patients who normally lived in London were discharged from the Consumption Hospital before death in order to spend their final days at home.

33 An exception to this rule is the London Hospital, where 16.9 per cent of deceased patients had lived outside London. In fact, many of these extra-metropolitan deaths were from districts such as Stratford, Canning Town, and West Ham, which were all just beyond the boundary of east London as defined by the Registrar-General.

34 The sectors are west, north, east, central and south London.

35 The exact proportions can be found in Mooney, Luckin and Tanner, 'Patient Pathways', Table 4, 247. A published analysis of the residential origins of patients attending King's College Hospital, Strand, showed that in 1856 almost 60 per cent of inpatients and just over 78 per cent of out-patients came from central London. Interestingly, a further 17.3 per cent of inpatients came from outside London, but only 1.3 per cent of outpatients. See King's College Hospital, *Report, 1856,* 18.

[36]   For example, in 1866 the London Hospital accepted cholera victims. Some general voluntary hospitals, such as the Royal Free Hospital in 1871, set up temporary infectious disease wards.

[37]   *24th Annual Report of the Registrar-General, 1861* (London, 1863), 208-10. The same source was used to estimate the cause of death structure for the 'outlying' workhouse deaths that were returned to their district of origin.

[38]   By the end of this time span, the number of metropolitan districts had been reduced from 36 to 30. According to the Registrar-General's classification, the deaths were allocated to the following categories of disease: smallpox, measles, scarlet fever, diphtheria, whooping cough, typhus (split into typhus and typhoid in 1869), cholera, diarrhoea and dysentery, respiratory tuberculosis and violent deaths.

[39]   Space does not permit analysis of other causes of death here, although various examples can be found in Mooney, Luckin and Tanner, 'Patient pathways', 263-69. Although it is by no means the most accurate measure of mortality, the crude death rate nevertheless broadly indicates the general level of health in an area, and as such it possessed a great deal of administrative and popular significance in the nineteenth century. See Mooney, 'Professionalization in public health'. It is calculated as the number of deaths per thousand living population.

[40]   Standard deviation measures how widely the crude death rates vary around the mean value.

[41]   Of course, Strand's very small resident population of 33,582 in 1881 means that the subtraction or addition of relatively few deaths has a significant impact on the mortality rate there.

Work, migration and the family: the example of Bethnal Green, 1891 to 1921

Kevin Schürer

Introduction

This chapter explores a number of inter-related themes using the community of Bethnal Green in London's East End at the end of the nineteenth and beginning of the twentieth century as a case study. As the title suggests, the investigation focuses on work, migration and family. The order of these three themes is not arbitrary. In this study migration forms a central link between an examination of the patterns of work observable within Bethnal Green on the one hand, and an examination of family forms and household structures on the other.

The relation between migration and employment opportunities–perceived or real–has long been established. The underlying importance of economic structures and strategies to migration flows has long been established. The link between the two was first emphasised in the pioneering work on migration by Ravenstein in the nineteenth century, and reiterated by Lee who suggested that the major causes of migration are economic.[1] However, in the literature dealing with historical migration flows there has been an over-concentration on the processes of migration and the examination of the characteristics of the migratory population, as opposed to the non-migratory population. Relatively little research has been undertaken on how migrant workers faired within the labour market once they had reached and settled within their place of destination. Literature on recent migration within the developing world has suggested that migrant workers are both disadvantaged and marginalised within the labour force.[2] This view of the position of migrant workers within the labour force stands in contrast to the theory of urban degeneration that originated in the mid to late nineteenth century and that prevailed in writings on the subject through to the early twentieth century. Within the context of London, the urban degeneration theory is most strongly put forward in the pioneering survey of the capital undertaken by Charles Booth and his co-workers and published during the 1890s.[3] In contrast to native Londoners, migrants to London, mainly drawn from rural areas, were depicted as being healthier, better skilled and exhibiting greater motivation. The native-born Londoners were seen to have been trapped within a cycle of degeneration. Their lot was characterised by low paid and intermittent work, in turn leading to poverty and deprivation. These conditions created a poor quality labour force amongst the London-born, which was passed on to and inherited by subsequent generations.[4] This model of urban degeneration has, however, been criticised, in particular by the historian Stedman Jones, who suggests that it is based on a spurious correlation in Booth's original investigations.[5] The theory of urban degeneration was used, Stedman Jones argues, to explain the observed correlation between levels of poverty across the London boroughs and the proportions born outside of London. This tended to mask the fact that migrants to London were disproportionately drawn to the areas of London with buoyant, fast-growing local economies, which were marked by lower levels of unemployment, less poverty and higher paid jobs. Conversely, migrants tended to avoid the poverty-stricken areas of London as places of destination. Importantly, the London-born themselves migrated from areas of poverty to areas that offered better employment prospects, and thus managed to break the urban degeneration cycle. More recently, the theory of urban degeneration has been re-examined by Hatton and Bailey in their study of working class migrants recorded in the New Survey of London Life and Labour, originally undertaken between 1929–31 under the guidance of Herbert Llewellyn-Smith.[6] Investigating the wage earnings of non-migrants, those migrating within London, and those migrating to the capital from beyond, the work of Hatton and Bailey would seem to support the general findings of Stedman Jones. They suggest that both migrants from outside London as well as migrants moving within London had a small but significant earnings advantage, but these can largely be accounted for in terms of differences in levels of skills. In conclusion they state that 'the London labour market does not seem to have discriminated between Londoners and non-Londoners or between migrants and non-migrants'. By concentrating on Bethnal Green, an area of London that was the destination point of many Jewish refugee migrants from eastern Europe in the late nineteenth and early twentieth centuries, this study develops the work of Hatton and Bailey by expanding the scope of the investigation to include a sizeable group of migrant workers from overseas.

The presence of this immigrant group within Bethnal Green also underpins a secondary focus to this study. Within studies of demographic, family and household structures in the past, at the macro level there is general acceptance of a broad dichotomy separating 'western' from 'eastern' Europe. The model upon which this is based was first formulated by Hajnal and has subsequently been developed by Laslett and others.[7] The basic characteristics of the model are that traditional Europe was separated roughly by a line running from St Petersburg in the north to Trieste in the south. To the east of this line marriage was early and near universal; the institution of service, a mechanism by which young adults left the parental home to join a migratory labour force prior to marriage, was virtually absent; and as a result households tended to be extended or complex in terms of structure. In contrast, the institution of service was commonplace in the west. As a result, marriage was late, being delayed until sufficient capital had been accumulated to establish an independent household, and the incidence of remaining unmarried was relatively high. Likewise, households tended to be simple or nuclear in structure, with extended or complex households resulting only in cases of 'extremis' where the nuclear family system failed due to unfavourable demographic or economic circumstances. Although there are a number of variations around this general model, and its applicability has been questioned for parts of southern and central Europe, it is still seen as valid as an explanatory tool in contrasting household systems geographically across Europe. To quote Alter, 'few generalisations in historical demography have had the influence or acceptance of the "Western European marriage pattern" described by John Hajnal'.[8] With reference to this model, this paper examines the household and demographic structures of the eastern European migrants in contrast to the native Bethnal Green population, as well other migrant groups.

The study area

Bethnal Green is well-known as a stereotypic 'traditional' working class area in the East End of London. This view of Bethnal Green owes much to the pioneering 1950s sociological study of the 'community' by Young (now Lord Young) and Willmott.[9] In their study the picture painted of Bethnal Green is of a traditional urban working-class community characterised by permanence and stability. Despite the forces of urban and economic development the watchword for Bethnal Green was continuity rather than change. The area was depicted as a tight-knit community in which the inhabitants grew up, married, raised families and worked within the confines of the local neighbourhood. The dissolution of family ties and social bonds which were generally believed to have been broken by the rapid urban development of post-war Britain were not evident in Bethnal Green. The working-class folk of Bethnal Green were found to cling loyally to the area in which they lived, often dismissing the outside world and the strangers that it brought. One woman interviewed by Young and Willmott, who had lived in the same house for 62 years, commented that her neighbours were 'new here—they've only been here eighteen years'.[10] Another old lady reported that when she went shopping she met in the course of a week no fewer than sixty people whom she recognised.[11] These views were confirmed by others who like Young and Willmott beat a path to Bethnal Green. For example, Robb summarised the situation as follows: 'Everyone is surrounded by people very much like himself, most of whom he has always known. Bethnal Green has many points of similarity with a village, or rather with a whole series of overlapping and interlocking villages. The opportunities for close, long term relationships is greater than is usually the case in a large metropolitan residential area'.[12]

The 'village' of Bethnal Green, however, caught the attention of social investigators long before Young and Willmott walked its streets. By the mid-nineteenth century Bethnal Green had already earned a reputation for itself as an area typified by abject poverty, poor housing, overcrowding and unemployment. This view was reinforced by Booth's survey of poverty in London undertaken towards the end of the century. This ranked Bethnal Green as the third poorest district in London, with some 51 per cent of the population in poverty.[13] One of the most notorious districts was the Old Nichol, situated on the boundary between Shoreditch and west Bethnal Green. The area was forcefully brought to public attention with the publication of Arthur Morrison's novel *A child of the Jago* for which the Old Nichol was used as a stage set.[14] The novel, which proved to be an instant success, also towed the urban degeneration line, telling the tale of Dicky Perrott, a child of the slum whose potential for upward mobility was halted by the corruption of the surrounding environment and his own heredity.[15] Perhaps what shocked the reading public most, however, was not the world of poverty that entrapped the Jago, but the culture of violence within which its inhabitants lived, and by which Dicky Perrott met his end, stabbed to death in a fight between neighbourhood gangs.

The association of the area with crime and 'immoral' living had earlier been fuelled by the infamous 'Whitechapel' murders that took place in the autumn of 1888.[16] The area's association with crime and immorality were as much a catalyst for slum clearance as public health and sanitary improvement. A new set of quite radical legal procedures governing slum clearance had been established in 1875 under the Conservative Home Secretary, Richard Cross.[17] The Act not only gave the government powers of compulsory purchase, but also allowed ratepayers and Medical Officers of Health to demand that housing be cleared if it could be proved that it was a risk to health.[18] One of the first clearance schemes to be approved was for Flower and Dean Street in Spitalfields, described as being 'perhaps the foulest and most dangerous street in the whole metropolis'.[19] Following this start, the newly-formed London County Council was at the end of the century to clear away the whole of the Old Nichol in the so-called Boundary Street Improvement Scheme. Indeed, this particular slum clearance forms a back-drop to Morrison's A child of the Jago, and ironically by the time Morrison's book was published in 1896 much of the Old Nichol had been swept away. However, pulling down slum buildings did not, in the short term at least, solve the problem. Due to the often prolonged nature of clearance and the difficulty of agreeing rebuilding plans, slum clearance tended to simply shift the problem elsewhere, often placing even further pressure on neighbouring areas that were already overcrowded.[20]

The situation of overcrowding in London's East End was exacerbated even further towards the end of the nineteenth century when the area was flooded by a wave of immigrants from eastern Europe. Arguably, this influx of people had a greater impact on the area than any programme of slum clearance and rebuilding. In his Introduction to the third series of his Life and labour, published in 1902, Charles Booth noted in relation to St George's in the East, just to the south-east of Bethnal Green, that since the area had first been surveyed in 1887, the most striking aspect of change was the growth in the number of Jews, occupying 'street after street'.[21] Following the assassination of Alexander II of Russia in March 1881, supposedly by a Jewish activist, a violent backlash against Jews erupted in many parts of the Empire. These physical attacks on Jews were followed by the May Laws of 1882 which brought in a series of pogroms that legalised discrimination against Jews in terms of both political and commercial freedoms.[22] It is estimated that in the next thirty or so years some 2 million Jews left Russia and its territories.[23] Three major waves, in 1882, 1891–2 and 1903–1906, coinciding with new government restrictions against the Jews and outbreaks of popular violence.[24] Of those leaving, many headed for England, seen as being both tolerant to religious minorities and freely open to immigrants. As one immigrant remarked, 'I left Russia and came to England because here Jews and Gentiles have no distinction made, they can live as brothers together'.[25] Also important was the fact that London was already home to a sizeable Jewish community.[26] However, quite how many of these 2 million settled in England is unclear since many used England, and London in particular, as a temporary staging post to other destinations, especially the United States.[27] This problem of estimating the size of the Jewish immigrant population was one recognised by contemporaries and has plagued students of the Jewish Diaspora ever since.[28] Pollins estimates that between 1880 and 1914 some 120,000 to 150,000 eastern European Jews settled in Britain.[29] Of these, the vast majority re-settled in London and most in the East End, only a short walk from the docks on the Isle of Dogs, where most would have disembarked.[30] Prior to 1881 the centre of London Jewry was in the eastern districts of the City of London, and neighbouring Whitechapel, St George's in the East and Mile End Old Town.[31] The first wave of immigrants saw the Jewish East End spread into Spitalfields, which became dominated by established immigrants and 'English' Jews with many of the new immigrants settling in Mile End New Town or Stepney. However, from the mid-1890s the immigrant settlers increasingly moved northwards into Bethnal Green. The 1911 census reveals that by this date 83 per cent of London's Russian and Russian Polish population was to be found in Stepney and Bethnal Green.[32]

Although the pace of Jewish immigration was already slowing down as the twentieth century dawned it virtually came to a halt following the passing of the Aliens Act of 1905.[33] This legislation which placed restrictions on immigration into the country for the first time since controls on immigration imposed during the wars with France were relaxed in 1826, came about as a direct result of the Jewish influx into London.[34] The arrival and settlement of large numbers of Jews from eastern Europe brought with it hostile reactions from several quarters. At one level the established middle class Jewish community of London, lead by a wealthy and aristocratic élite headed by the Rothschild family, did not look entirely favourably on the flood of poor Jews arriving in London as they feared that any resulting anti-Semitic back-lash would rebound on the Jewish community as a whole and would thus undermine their place within society.[35] Rather than government intervention, London's middle-class Jewish élite preferred to see the situation as a 'Jewish problem' that should be solved within and by the Jewish community.[36] Indeed, much was done by the charitable Jewish Board of Guardians and the Russian-Jewish Committee to both relieve poverty amongst the immigrant Jews and aid repatriation and emigration to America.[37] It is estimated that between 1880 and 1914 some 50,000 were provided with aid to emigrate from London to the United States, or to return to Russia.[38] The Jewish Board of Guardians and other charities also assisted in finding the immigrants accommodation. Lord Rothschild personally oversaw and heavily financed a programme for the construction of new model dwellings for immigrant families in the East End.[39] For the Jewish élite the best solution was for the immigrants to become 'English', like themselves, and as quickly as possible.[40]

Despite the best endeavours of London's middle-class Jewish community to relieve the pressures that the flood of immigrants placed on the East End, resentment among the native population soon grew. Opposition towards the new Jewish settlers was particularly evident amongst the rate-paying lower middle classes of the East End.[41] For them, the eastern European influx brought with it further overcrowding and additional pressures on sanitation, both of which pushed up the cost of the local rates. The level of rates in the London Borough of Stepney increased by some fifty per cent between 1890 and 1906 and in 1901 the local *Eastern Post* newspaper noted that the inhabitants of Stepney were 'groaning under the burden of rates and taxes'.[42] The voices of the rate-paying lower middle classes were also joined by members of the working classes who not only suffered from increased rents due to the lack of available local accommodation, but also blamed their worsening employment prospects on the immigrants by working for lower wage rates. The protests soon became part of a hotly contested political issue over immigration control, and in an attempt to stem the tide of protest the Conservative government established a Royal Commission on Alien Immigration to investigate the problem.[43] When this eventually reported in 1903 it concluded that the lack of control on immigration into the country lead to the spread of disease, criminality and anarchists and recommended the enactment of legislation to restrict certain types of immigration, principally those in which migrants were unable to demonstrate that they were capable of supporting themselves and their families.[44] The result was the passing of the Aliens Act in 1905. This proved to be an almost immediate success, not only drastically cutting the numbers of immigrants entering the country but also due to the power of deterrent, doing so at minimal expense. As a result the number of immigrants arriving from Russia fell from 12,481 to 4,223 in the four years between 1906 and 1910, with comparatively few being turned away, a total of just 4,176 in the same period.[45]

Data sources

One of the key sources for studying patterns of employment and the family is the decennial census, taken in England and Wales since 1801.[46] Although the published returns of the census provide much information, this is in a highly aggregate form, and usually at a relatively high level of geography. Thus, to address the issues posed in this chapter, one needs recourse to the individual and household level data provided in the original census enumerators' books.[47] However, these are closed to public inspection for a period of 100 years. Fortunately, for this paper it has been possible to make use of a selection of anonymised individual level census data created by the Office for National Statistics (ONS–the then Office of Population, Censuses and Surveys)[48] for the Cambridge Group for the History of Population and Social Structure.[49] These data cover the four decadal census years between 1891 and 1921 and have been stripped of both names and addresses by ONS, thus preventing the identification of individuals. The Bethnal Green census materials are one of thirteen areas or locales selected across England and Wales from the four census years.[50] The minimum unit for selection was a census enumeration district and each locale is composed of a cluster of usually contiguous enumeration districts. Unfortunately the boundaries of enumeration districts can vary from census to census, especially in urban areas. Thus within each locale enumeration districts were grouped together in order to form areas for which the geographical territory covered is reasonably constant over time. Thus in the case of the Bethnal Green sample, a selection of enumeration districts drawn from the Registration District of Bethnal Green were computerised by ONS covering roughly the same collection of streets in each of the four census years. However, in order to preserve confidentiality, the identification and location of these streets within the Registration District is unknown. The overall size of the population available from the Bethnal Green sample is given in Table 1. This shows that the numbers available for analysis range from just over 8,000 in 1891 to a little under 13,000 for 1901. These totals do not reflect the general underlying population trends of Bethnal Green as a whole, but rather the changing matrix of streets within the enumeration districts that constitute the sample. Throughout the period, the population of the London Borough of Bethnal Green declined by 9 per cent from some 129,000 in 1891 to 117,000 in 1921.[51]

	population	n. of EDs	n. of households
1891	8,101	6	1,782
1901	12,797	7	2,789
1911	10,878	6	2,305
1921	9,080	8	2,086

Table 1. Size of the Bethnal Green sample, by census year

Analysis

The research presented in this paper is principally based on a comparative analysis of the anonymised census data. For each year the individuals recorded within the census data have been assigned to one of four 'migrant' groups: the Jewish settlers in Bethnal Green; those 'native' to Bethnal Green; other 'Londoners' living in Bethnal Green; and those migrant to London travelling from within the United Kingdom. The work and family experiences of the Bethnal Green population is examined and compared across each of these four groups. However, before turning to the results of these analyses, it is appropriate to outline how each of these groups has been defined.

Unlike most other countries, the census of England and Wales has never included a question on religion.[52] In the absence of such a question it is not easy to identify 'ethnic' groups within the nineteenth century censuses.[53] In order to determine which individuals recorded in the census enumerators' books are Jewish, one might recourse to the recorded surnames and personal names,[54] however, since the available sample data are anonymised this possibility does not exist. Instead, given that the Jewish immigrants of late-nineteenth and early twentieth-century Bethnal Green were mainly of eastern European origin, the individual's given place of birth has been used as a surrogate indicator. Like all surrogate measures, this is not without its problems. Undoubtedly there will be some Jews recorded in the Bethnal Green sample whose origins are not eastern European.[55] Likewise, there may well be some eastern Europeans in the sample data who are not Jewish, perhaps even including the occasional person who was born in eastern Europe but whose family background and up-bringing occurred elsewhere. Thus, the group identified by birthplace in the census data should more strictly be referred as 'those of eastern European origin by birth, the vast majority of whom are Jewish', however, throughout this paper the terms 'Jewish' and 'eastern European' shall be used as a convenient shorthand.

Two other points need to be made. First, what constitutes eastern Europe? Using the places of birth recorded in the census enumerators' books, 'eastern' has been defined as all those stated as being born within the Russian Empire during the period 1891 to 1921, including much of present-day Poland, the Baltic States, Belarus and Ukraine. In addition, Romania, which was an independent kingdom from 1881 has been included within the definition, as well as Moldavia which was then a principality within Romania. The inclusion of Romania is important since many Jews fled Romania during this period following explosion and persecution. The situation of Austria is rather more problematic. During the period of study the Austro-Hungarian Empire stretched across a large territory in central and eastern Europe, from the borders of Switzerland to Serbia and beyond. However, in those cases where place as well as country of birth are recorded in the census, most of the Austrian examples are drawn from provinces in the east and north-east of the Empire, now in present-day Poland, Ukraine and Romania. For this reason, those recording their birthplace as 'Austria' have been included within the eastern European definition. A second problem arises from the fact that in the years after settlement in London, newborn children of the immigrant group will obviously be recorded in the census with a 'native' birthplace. In consequence, all such 'second-generation' migrants were treated as eastern European rather than native Londoners.[56]

Defining and identifying the other three 'migrant' groups analysed in this study proved to be less problematic. In defining the 'native' Bethnal Green population the net was thrown slightly wider to include the neighbouring districts of Shoreditch, Spitalfields, Stepney, Mile End and Canning Town, if only because it is likely that the perceived boundaries between them were relatively fluid. Other 'Londoners' were classed as those born outside of the wider Bethnal Green area, yet still within London, including those parts of metropolitan Middlesex, Kent and Surrey. Likewise, those classed as 'UK born' are those with birthplaces within the UK not identified as being from either Bethnal Green or London. This left a small residual of people who were born outside of the UK, but not within eastern Europe, as previously defined, together with those whose place of birth went unrecorded or could not be determined. This group was numerically very small and was discounted from the analyses that follow. For each of the three UK-born 'migrant' groups, second generation migrants were, as in the case of the Jews discussed above, counted within the parental migrant group.

Lastly, it should be noted that although these four groups are used in the subsequent analyses as a basis of comparison, it would be wrong to assume homogeneity across any particular group. Although the migrants from eastern Europe most probably shared a common religion, it would be wrong to view them as a single entity. Despite being united by Judaism and the fact that they had been up-rooted from their homelands, they spoke different languages and had different national traditions. Whilst those in England, especially those in the East End, saw them very much as a single mass, the Jews were very aware of the differences between them. As one child of an immigrant family (from Lithuania) remarked: 'There were divisions. The Austrian Jews were looked upon as not necessarily haughty—but bad tempered. The Rumanians—they were selfish. The Polish—I suppose there were some differences because the accent was very different....And the Litvaks [Lithuanians] were looked upon as the intellectuals'.[57] Similarly, yet on a rather different scale, the group labelled as 'born in UK, outside London' is a very mixed bag. This group includes people drawn from many different parts of the kingdom, including Scotland and Ireland, however, most were from England, originating from rural counties.

	1891 n.	%	1901 n.	%	1911 n.	%	1921 n.	%
Bethnal Green born	4,992	61.6	9,014	70.4	6,617	60.8	5,328	58.7
Born outside London (UK)	1,234	15.2	1,173	9.2	1,196	11.0	594	6.5
Born eastern Europe	63	0.8	554	4.3	1,041	9.6	909	10.0
Born elsewhere in London	1,731	21.4	1,929	15.1	1,962	18.0	2,176	24.0
Birthplace unclear	81	1.0	127	1.6	62	0.8	73	0.9
Totals	8,101	100.0	12,797	100.0	10,878	100.0	9,080	100.0

Table 2. Size of the 'migrant' groups: Bethnal Green, 1891–1921

The relative size of these four groups is provided in Table 2. From this it can be seen that the native Bethnal Greeners formed the majority in each of the four census years, normally being about sixty per cent of the resident population. The Jewish sector of the population increased proportionally over time. In 1891 their numbers were small, being less than one per cent of the total, then the size of this group rose quickly to reach around ten per cent in both 1911 and 1921. The small size of the group in the first of the census years means that it is inappropriate to draw comparisons between the Jews and others prior to 1901. The Londoners were the second largest group varying between fifteen per cent of the population in 1901 and nearly a quarter in 1921. Those born elsewhere in the UK formed their largest proportional share in 1891, accounting for fifteen per cent of the resident population, but decline in relative terms as the Jews become numerically more important, falling to just six per cent in 1921.

In addition to the changing relative sizes of the four groups, it is important also to consider the age and sex distributions of the groups. These are given in Table 3. As might be expected, given the demographic characteristics of most migrant groups, the native Bethnal Greeners tended to be 'younger' than either of the other three sections of the population, usually with some forty per cent being aged under twenty. At the other end of the spectrum, the Jews tended to be more 'middle aged', with some seventy per cent of their number being aged between twenty and fifty. Between these two extremes, unsurprisingly, the Londoners were more like those from Bethnal Green in terms of their age profile, yet not quite so youthful, while those born outside of London, were more like the Jews, yet with higher numbers under twenty and fewer in middle age. Interestingly, however, those born outside of London displayed relatively large proportions of people in old age, aged sixty-five or over. It would seem unlikely that this group were recent arrivals to the area and is probably a resulting feature of earlier migrant flows into London's East End. In terms of gender it is perhaps a little surprising that the numbers of males and females are evenly distributed across the four groups. None of the migrant streams displayed a clear propensity toward either sex. Clearly, both the differing relative sizes of the four groups under observation, together with their variant age structures must be taken into when considering the underlying patterns of work and family across the four groups.

Work

Bethnal Green had a very varied occupational structure; a range of different occupations was present and none clearly dominated. Figure 1 also shows that the profile and relative distribution of occupations undertaken by males changed little over the course of the thirty years covered by the four censuses. In the early decades of the nineteenth century Bethnal Green had been a centre for much of London's silk weaving industry but this was already in decline by the mid-century and by the end of the century had all but disappeared.[58] In its place London's East End established a tradition as being the home of 'sweated' trades, in particular the manufacture of clothing.[59] However, as Figure 1 illustrates, to concentrate purely on the sweated trades, notorious though they may have been, is to lose sight of the wider picture. Throughout the period under investigation employment in the production of furniture, preparation of food and drink, construction and dock-working were for men equal to if not more important as a source of employment.[60]

However, in the case of female employment, Figure 2 shows that female employment was more concentrated in a smaller range of occupations and displayed less variance of experience than male

1891

Males

	0-19 n.	0-19 %	20-34 n.	20-34 %	35-49 n.	35-49 %	50-64 n.	50-64 %	65+ n.	65+ %	Total n.	Total %
Bethnal Green born	1,442	59.0	550	22.5	285	11.7	121	4.9	48	2.0	2,446	100
Born outside London (UK)	142	22.9	174	28.0	182	29.3	102	16.4	21	3.4	621	100
Born eastern Europe	8	20.0	15	37.5	7	17.5	6	15.0	4	10.0	40	100
Born elsewhere in London	390	46.1	217	25.7	161	19.0	62	7.3	16	1.9	846	100

Females

	0-19 n.	0-19 %	20-34 n.	20-34 %	35-49 n.	35-49 %	50-64 n.	50-64 %	65+ n.	65+ %	Total n.	Total %
Bethnal Green born	1,498	58.8	531	20.9	275	10.8	175	6.9	67	2.6	2,546	100
Born outside London (UK)	148	24.1	164	26.8	177	28.9	92	15.0	32	5.2	613	100
Born eastern Europe	6	26.1	11	47.8	1	4.3	5	21.7	0	0.0	23	100
Born elsewhere in London	353	39.9	220	24.9	183	20.7	85	9.6	44	5.0	885	100

1901

Males

	0-19 n.	0-19 %	20-34 n.	20-34 %	35-49 n.	35-49 %	50-64 n.	50-64 %	65+ n.	65+ %	Total n.	Total %
Bethnal Green born	2,580	59.4	925	21.3	551	12.7	245	5.6	45	1.0	4,346	100
Born outside London (UK)	57	9.7	201	34.1	168	28.5	118	20.0	45	7.6	589	100
Born eastern Europe	83	27.3	137	45.1	73	24.0	7	2.3	4	1.3	304	100
Born elsewhere in London	345	36.1	298	31.2	194	20.3	98	10.3	20	2.1	955	100

Females

	0-19 n.	0-19 %	20-34 n.	20-34 %	35-49 n.	35-49 %	50-64 n.	50-64 %	65+ n.	65+ %	Total n.	Total %
Bethnal Green born	2,634	56.4	1,079	23.1	573	12.3	282	6.0	100	2.1	4,668	100
Born outside London (UK)	73	12.5	159	27.2	171	29.3	142	24.3	39	6.7	584	100
Born eastern Europe	88	35.2	98	39.2	50	20.0	12	4.8	2	0.8	250	100
Born elsewhere in London	316	32.4	271	27.8	232	23.8	112	11.5	43	4.4	974	100

1911

Males

	0-19		20-34		35-49		50-64		65+		Total	
	n.	%	n.	%	n.	%	n.	%	n.	%	n.	%
Bethnal Green born	1,925	59.3	689	21.2	405	12.5	183	5.6	45	1.4	3,247	100
Born outside London (UK)	195	33.6	123	21.2	145	25.0	87	15.0	31	5.3	581	100
Born eastern Europe	119	22.2	214	39.9	154	28.7	40	7.5	9	1.7	536	100
Born elsewhere in London	450	45.6	227	23.0	193	19.6	83	8.4	33	3.3	986	100

Females

	0-19		20-34		35-49		50-64		65+		Total	
	n.	%	n.	%	n.	%	n.	%	n.	%	n.	%
Bethnal Green born	1,902	56.4	741	22.0	447	13.3	194	5.8	86	2.6	3,370	100
Born outside London (UK)	195	31.7	132	21.5	145	23.6	99	16.1	44	7.2	615	100
Born eastern Europe	102	20.2	201	39.8	162	32.1	34	6.7	6	1.2	505	100
Born elsewhere in London	419	42.9	244	25.0	178	18.2	104	10.7	31	3.2	976	100

1921

Males

	0-19		20-34		35-49		50-64		65+		Total	
	n.	%	n.	%	n.	%	n.	%	n.	%	n.	%
Bethnal Green born	1,443	56.7	534	21.0	335	13.2	176	6.9	56	2.2	2,544	100
Born outside London (UK)	87	31.3	38	13.7	79	28.4	54	19.4	20	7.2	278	100
Born eastern Europe	31	7.3	96	22.5	189	44.4	91	21.4	19	4.5	426	100
Born elsewhere in London	487	46.0	232	21.9	200	18.9	110	10.4	30	2.8	1059	100

Females

	0-19		20-34		35-49		50-64		65+		Total	
	n.	%	n.	%	n.	%	n.	%	n.	%	n.	%
Bethnal Green born	1,512	54.3	624	22.4	386	13.9	184	6.6	78	2.8	2,784	100
Born outside London (UK)	99	31.3	55	17.4	71	22.5	47	14.9	44	13.9	316	100
Born eastern Europe	48	9.9	143	29.6	194	40.2	87	18.0	11	2.3	483	100
Born elsewhere in London	485	43.4	258	23.1	210	18.8	110	9.8	54	4.8	1,117	100

Table 3. Age and sex structure of the 'migrant' groups: Bethnal Green, 1891-1921

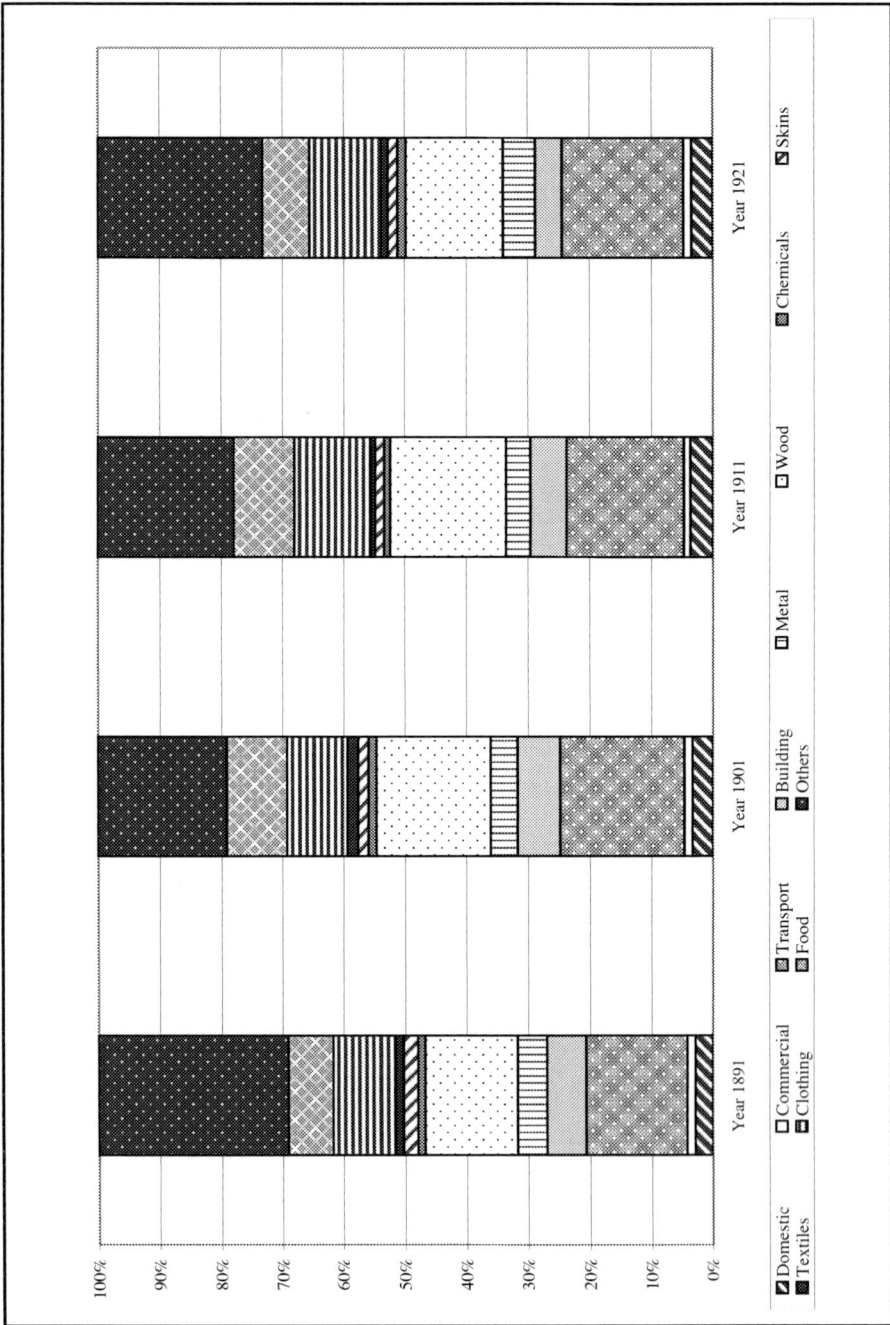

Figure 1. Male occupations: 1891 to 1921

Legend: Domestic, Textiles, Commercial, Clothing, Transport, Food, Building, Others, Metal, Wood, Chemicals, Skins

Year 1891, Year 1901, Year 1911, Year 1921

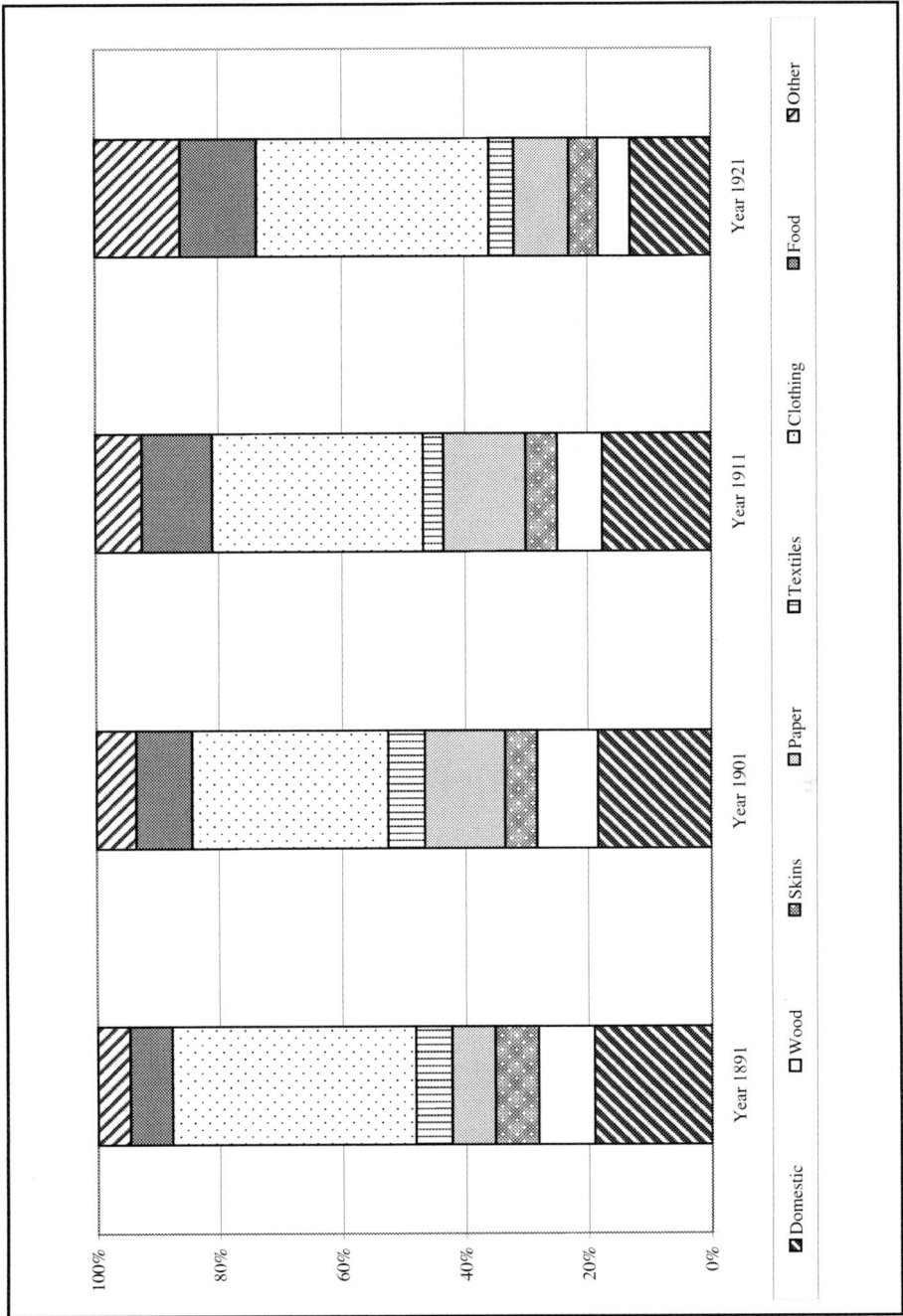

Figure 2. Female occupations: 1891 to 1921

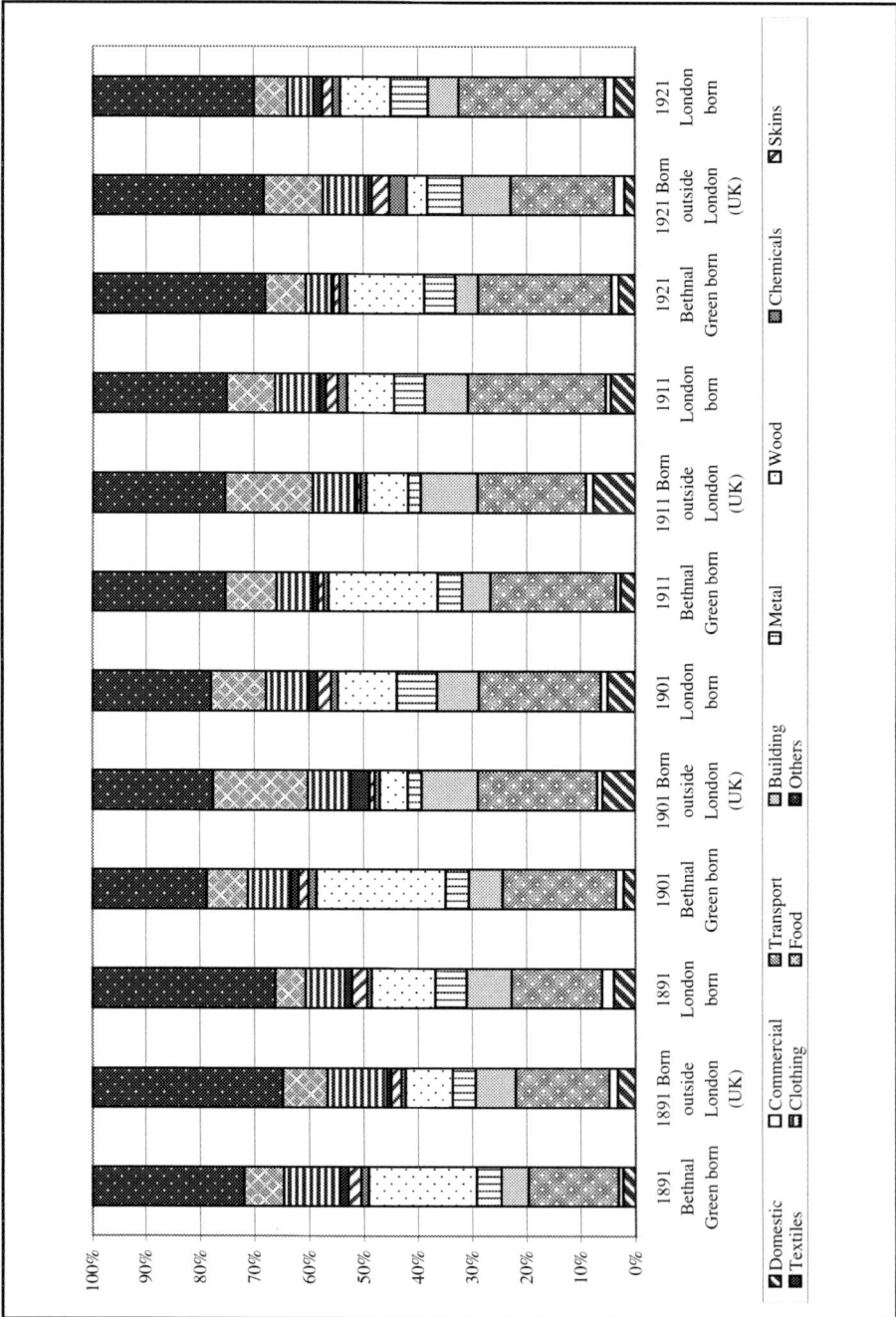

Figure 3. Male occupations: 'migrant' groups, 1891 to 1921

Legend:
- Domestic
- Textiles
- Commercial
- Clothing
- Transport
- Food
- Building
- Others
- Metal
- Wood
- Chemicals
- Skins

X-axis categories: 1891 Bethnal Green born, 1891 Born outside London (UK), 1891 London born, 1901 Bethnal Green born, 1901 Born outside London (UK), 1901 London born, 1911 Bethnal Green born, 1911 Born outside London (UK), 1911 London born, 1921 Bethnal Green born, 1921 Born outside London (UK), 1921 London born

Y-axis: 0% to 100%

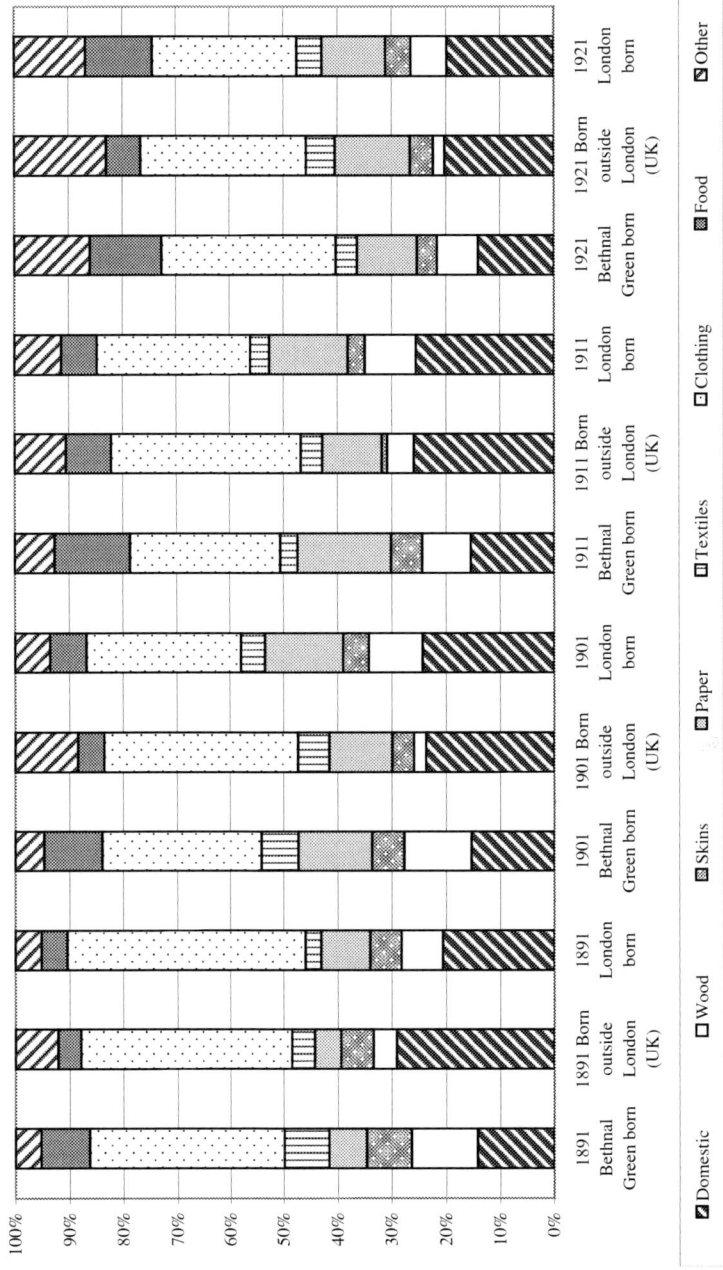

Figure 4. Female occupations: 'migrant' groups, 1891 to 1921

employment. In particular, the manufacturing of clothing proved to be the single largest occupation for women throughout the period, accounting for between twenty and fifteen per cent of all female employment. In this regard, the sweated trades were a more important structural element of female labour force than the male labour force. Likewise, home-working undoubtedly formed a more important for the female labour force than for men. Domestic service was the second largest employment source for women, but declined gradually in importance over the period, from a high of some ten per cent in 1891 to around seven per cent in 1921. This decline in domestic service was compensated by an increase over the period in the numbers employed in the preparation of food (from some four to seven per cent) and those employed in a variety of 'other' occupations (from three to eight per cent).

Turning to the occupational structures of the different migrant groups, the situation of males is shown in Figure 3. Given the relative size of the group, it is not surprising to find that the occupational profile of the local Bethnal Green born resembles quite closely that of the overall area shown in Figure 1 and discussed above. Moreover, this is an occupational structure largely shared by both the London and UK migrants. Differences can be seen, especially between those originating from outside of London and those from both Bethnal Green and London as a whole, but these differences are slight. Such uniformity in occupational structure would seem to question the operation of urban degeneration in this period. However, it is worth noting that the male migrants from outside London do record slightly higher proportions employed in building construction work and employment in transport, mainly in the docks. Equally, in 1921 migrants from outside of London were disproportionately employed in greater numbers in the growing chemical industries. Likewise, fewer found employment in the wood-based furniture-making industry, more traditional to the Bethnal Green area.

Turning to the situation of females, Figure 4, although the general trend, as with males, is a pattern of general similarity between the Bethnal Green born, other London-born and those born outside of London, differences can be seen. The local native-born females tended to be employed in domestic service to a lesser extent than either of the other two migrant groups. Over all four census years, the proportions of Bethnal Green born females employed in domestic service remained at a constant rate of between 14 and 15 per cent. In comparison, in 1891 some 30 per cent of females born outside of London were employed in service while 20 per cent of the London-born were thus employed. Thereafter, the London-born and those born outside of London were employed in service in roughly similar proportions: 23 per cent in 1901, and 25 and 20 per cent in 1911 and 1921, respectively. Equally, those females born outside of London tended, with the exception of the final year of investigation, to be employed more frequently in the manufacturing of clothing than their native Bethnal Green counterparts. This was especially true of 1901 and 1911 when, for both census years, 34 per cent of those born outside of London were employed in clothing compared to some 28 per cent of Bethnal Green born females. In these two years the levels of females born in London employed in clothing were at similar levels to the native Bethnal Green females, however, in 1891 London-born females recorded the highest levels working in the manufacture of clothing, being 43 per cent compared to the Bethnal Green figure of 36 per cent. In compensation for the lower numbers of local Bethnal Green women employed in both domestic service and the manufacture of clothing, slightly greater numbers were employed the preparation of food, wood-based industries and the manufacture of textiles than either the London-born or those migrants born outside of London. It can also be noted that the proportion of women employed in paper-based industries increased significantly between 1891 and 1901, effecting all three birthplace groups.

	1890	1902	1910	1920
Building trades				
Bricklayers	38s 7d	44s 11d	42s 5d	102s 8d
Carpenters and joiners	38s 3d	44s 11d	42s 5d	102s 8d
Labourers	25s 6d	28s 9d	28s 3½d	91s 8d
Woodworking				
Cabinet makers	40s 6d	43s 9d	43s 9d	107s 9d
French polishers	37s 0d	39s 5d	39s 5d	107s 9d
Upholsterers	-	46s 11d	46s 11d	107s 9d
Transport				
Dock labourers*	5s	5s	5s 10d	16s 0d
Carters	-	25s 0d	26s 0d	66s 0d

Table 4. Weekly wage rates in London, 1890 to 1920
Source: Llewellyn Smith, ed., New Survey, vol. I, pp.136–7.
*Note: * = Wages of dock labourers employed by the Port of London Authority, per day, calculated on a 10-hour a day basis.*

It is impossible to say from census data if the migrants, either from within London, or without, earned higher or lower wages than the non-migrant locals. However, in this regard it is instructive to view the occupational structure of the migrants groups alongside the figures in Table 4 which gives average wage rates in London for key male occupations. This would suggest that, in direct contradiction to the urban degeneration theory, in the case of Bethnal Green, migrants moving to the area from outside of London found work in slightly greater numbers *pro rata* within the lower paid sectors of the work force, compared with the native born and migrants from within London. The key exception to this rule were those who moved to the area at the end of the period to work in the newly-emerging chemical industry and tended to enjoy higher wage rates.[61] In some respects the same is also true of female employment. As noted above migrant women displayed a greater propensity to be working in the manufacture of clothing and domestic service, both relatively poorly paid, in comparison with the native Bethnal Greeners. In attempting to determine how well the migrant labour force fared relative to native workers, it is also instructive to examine the numbers out of work. Unlike previous censuses that of 1921 explicitly recorded information on those currently out of work at the time of the census enumeration.[62] The proportions of males recorded as out of work in 1921, by age group, are provided in Table 5. This reveals some interesting differences between the various birthplace groups. For males aged between 20–24 the native Bethnal Greeners recorded lower rates of unemployment than either the migrants born within London or those born outside. However, for those aged 30–39 and 45–49 this pattern was reversed, while for those aged 35–39 the proportions were broadly similar. These trends in unemployment may be suggestive of a general pattern in which the younger migrants new to the area found it harder to gain permanent employment, however once settled they displayed a marginal employment advantage over the native Bethnal Green workers. Alternatively, the figures in Table 5 might be explained by older migrants, perhaps more experienced and better skilled, getting along better than younger migrants as well as their local born contemporaries.

Thus, based on the comparative occupational structures of Bethnal Green, discussed above, it is difficult to find clear evidence to support the general notion that migrants were better paid and better placed within the labour market. In support of the work by Hatton and Bailey, it would appear that the differences between those moving from within London and those coming from further afield within the UK were slim. Indeed, the overwhelming picture is one of similarity between both sets of migrants and the native-born of Bethnal Green. Some migrants, as indicated by the chemical workers, probably displayed greater skill levels and were therefore better paid. Yet these were more than compensated for by others who found work in more casual employment in the construction industry and the docks, work which was not only more poorly paid but also more peripatetic in nature, often resulting in periods of unemployment or under-employment. However, the age-specific unemployment data presented for 1921 (Table 5) indicate that life-cycle was also an important feature. It may be that young newly-arrived migrants were worse placed than locals within the labour market, but over time experienced comparatively greater upward social mobility. Alternatively, or working in combination with this feature, older migrants were marginally less likely to be unemployed than local workers of the same age. The overall experience of Bethnal Green demonstrates that in terms of the labour market migrants cannot be looked upon as a homogenous group. Some may have been better skilled, but others were clearly not.

| Age | Percentage | | | |
	Bethnal Green born	Born elsewhere in London	Born within UK, outside London	Eastern European born
20-24	18	24	28	18
25-29	20	19	16	16
30-34	14	12	12	9
35-39	10	9	10	7
40-44	12	7	15	9
45-49	10	7	7	9

Table 5. Proportions not working by age and migrant group: males, 1921

The case of the Jewish influx into Bethnal Green also demonstrates clearly that the experience of migration and its impact on the labour market was far from uniform. In the evidence presented to the Royal Commission on Alien Immigration, a common complaint levied at the recent Jewish immigrants was that they created economic hardship for the native population not so much because of the resulting saturation of the labour market but because they worked for longer hours and for less wages than any native worker could, or would. This was not just competition, this was unfair competition. As one boot and shoe maker complained, 'a respectable and honest man that wants to get an honest living and bring up his family could never compete with them', one of his employees adding 'they work so much cheaper than the native workmen do...it affects anyone who wants to live decent, because they could never live decent on the price that these aliens earn for their weekly wage'.[63] Equally, Charles Booth commented that the 'unfortunate East End worker, struggling to support his family and keep the wolf from the door, has to contend with all these forms of competition. He is met and vanquished by the Jew fresh from Poland or Russia, accustomed to a lower standard of life, and above all of food, than would be possible to a native of these islands; less skilled and perhaps less strong, but in his way more fit—pliant, adaptable, patient, adroit.'[64] The latter part of this quote provides an indication of a rather different representation of the Jewish immigrant worker. Rather than being cheap and under-cutting, in her essay on 'The Jewish community', as part of Booth's survey of *Life and labour,* Beatrice Potter portrayed the Jew as 'economic man' personified. She praised his hard-working nature, his commercial instincts, his family values and his temperance, which together enabled and quickened his upward social and economic mobility.[65] 'Besides the possession of a trained intellect, admirably adapted to commerce and finance, there is another...more important factor in the Jew's success. From birth upwards, the pious Israelite (male and female) is subjected to a moral and physical regimen, which, while it favours the full development of the bodily organs, protects them from abuse and disease, and stimulates the growth of physical self-control and mental endurance'.[66] To Potter, the Jewish immigrant did not so much present a case of unfair competition, but rather ability over inability, or as she put it: 'In the Jewish inhabitants of East London we see therefore a race of brain-workers competing with a class of manual labourers'.[67]

Unlike other male migrants to Bethnal Green in this period, for whom, as has been discussed above, the occupational profiles varied relatively little from the indigenous population, the Jewish migrants from eastern Europe displayed a distinctive occupational structure. As shown in Figure 5, employment amongst the Jewish immigrant population was heavily dominated by just two occupations: the manufacture of clothing and wood-based industries, especially cabinet-making and the manufacture of other furniture. Taken together, these two main

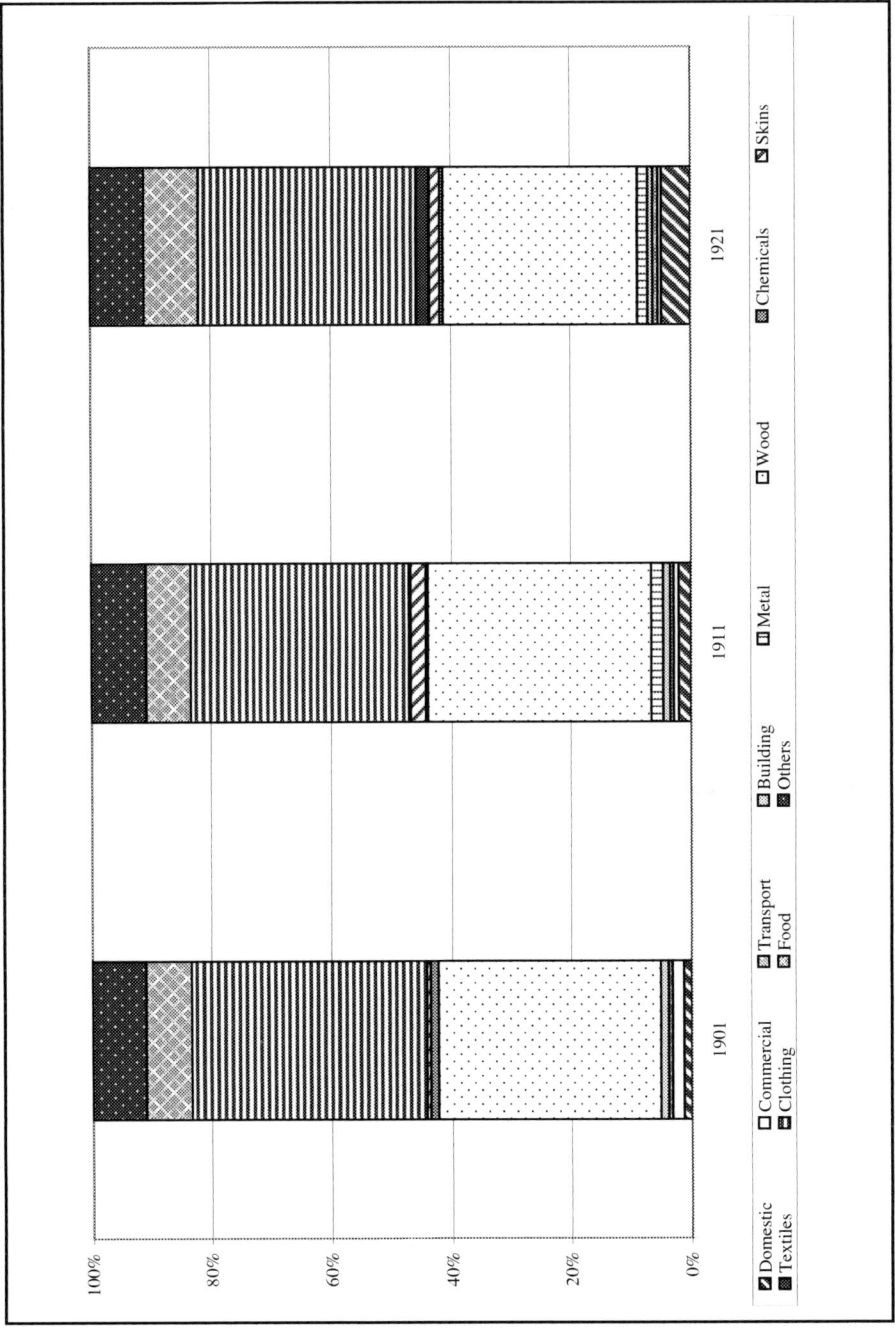

Figure 5. Male occupations: east European born, 1901 to 1921

Legend:
- Domestic
- Commercial
- Transport
- Building
- Metal
- Wood
- Chemicals
- Skins
- Textiles
- Clothing
- Food
- Others

Axis years: 1901, 1911, 1921

occupations employed between some seventy-five and eighty per cent of the Jewish male labour force over the period 1901 to 1921, in roughly equal proportions. This heavy concentration of employment, dependent on just two key occupational sectors, is not perhaps overly surprising. Contemporary studies on Jewish occupational structures throughout Europe demonstrated the extent to which employment within the Jewish population was highly concentrated within a relatively limited range of occupations.[68] In part, this concentration of occupational activity was itself the result of traditional restrictions on the activities of Jews enforced at both governmental level and within bodies regulating the internal organisation of certain trades. In consequence, Jewish employment became concentrated and developed specialisation within a limited number of activities which were largely unregulated, or loosely controlled by traditional guilds or unions.[69]

				Percentage			
	Males				Females		
In parental home		Outside parental home		In parental home		Outside parental home	
not working	working	not working	working	not working	working	not working	working
Bethnal Green born							
1901							
15-19	6	85	1	8	12	74	2	12
20-24	2	55	0	43	5	45	38	12
25-29	0	25	0	75	2	17	71	10
1921							
15-19	17	72	1	10	17	70	5	8
20-24	11	50	7	32	13	45	30	12
25-29	8	20	12	60	8	15	62	15
Eastern European born							
1901							
15-19	14	60	2	24	8	60	15	17
20-24	2	15	3	80	5	25	58	12
25-29	0	5	0	95	5	10	75	10
1921							
15-19	16	85	0	9	20	80	0	0
20-24	18	68	0	4	15	72	10	3
25-29	12	30	4	54	9	35	41	15

Table 6. Work and patterns of residence: Bethnal Green born and eastern European born, 1901 and 1921

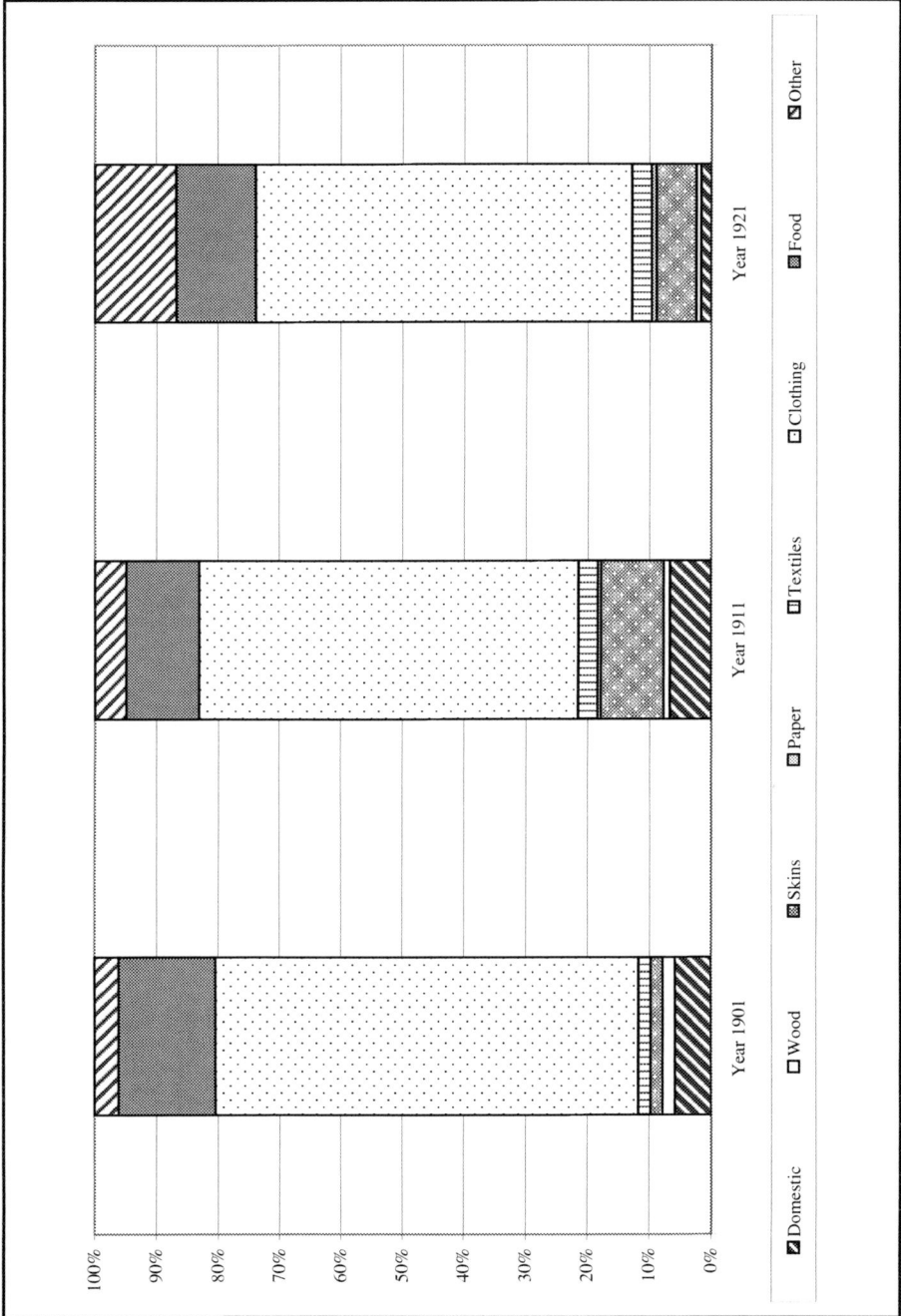

Figure 6. Female occupations: east European born, 1901 to 1921

Legend: Domestic, Wood, Skins, Paper, Textiles, Clothing, Food, Other

In the light of the complains made against the Jewish immigrant workers by 'native' workers, and the claims of 'unfair' competition, mentioned previously, given the occupational profile of the Jewish workers, such claims were only valid in the case of just two sectors of the local economy – the manufacture of clothing and furniture. Thus open competition between the Jews and the native workers could neither be seen as general nor widespread. Only a relatively small minority of the native work force could be seen to be threatened by the eastern European immigration. However, in considering the nature of competition within this minority group, it is important to picture the employment of women alongside men. In comparison to the situation of male employment, Figure 6 shows that the occupations of eastern European women were heavily dominated throughout the period by employment in the manufacture of clothing, with some two-thirds of Jewish women recorded as working in this trade. Thus, in combination with their male counterparts, that the Jewish immigrants did form a major source of competition to local native workers employed in the clothing industry. However, in this regard, it is also interesting to note that the structure of employment within the Jewish immigrant population underwent a rapid and significant shift following their settlement in the East End. With reference to Table 6, it can be seen that in 1901 of those aged between 15–19, 85 per cent of Bethnal Green born males were recorded as working and living in the parental home, compared to just 60 per cent of Jewish immigrants. The respective figures for females being 74 and 60 per cent. Moreover, 14 per cent of the Jewish males in this age group were recorded as living in the parental home and not working, compared to just 6 per cent of the native born. Of those aged 20–24, 55 per cent of Bethnal Green males were employed and still living at home compared to just 15 per cent of Jewish males of the same age. For females, the comparative figures were 45 and 25 per cent, respectively. Of all females aged 20–24, 57 per cent of the native born were working against only 37 per cent of the eastern European immigrants. This suggests that at this date Jews were marrying earlier than those from Bethnal Green and consequently moving out of the parental home earlier, but also that of those who remained in the parental home fewer children tended to work in Jewish households than in those of local families, and Jewish women tended overall to be less likely to be working than local women. It should also be noted that whilst

Table 6 compares just the experience of eastern Europeans against the Bethnal Green born, the patterns displayed by those born elsewhere within London and those born outside of London were broadly similar to those of the native Bethnal Green families. However, twenty years on the situation had changed quite dramatically. By 1921 Jewish children were staying in the parental home longer and displayed a greater tendency, compared to the children of local native families, to be working.[70] Equally, Jewish wives and daughters also now worked in greater numbers than their local-born counterparts. Indeed, the turn-about is quite striking. Of those aged between 20–24 of eastern European origin 68 per cent of males and 72 per cent of females were recorded as still living in the parental home and working compared with just 50 and 45 per cent of the Bethnal Green born, respectively. Moreover, of this age group 75 per cent of Jewish women were working against 57 per cent of native Bethnal Green women. For the next age group, those aged 25–29, 30 and 35 per cent of the eastern European males and females respectively were still living in the parental home and working compared with just 20 and 15 per cent of the Bethnal Green born. Less than a third of the local born women aged 25–29 worked against a half of all Jewish women of the same age. Over the course of the first twenty years of the century, the Jewish immigrants found a way to compete with the native work force, not so much working for lower wages *per se*, but rather by retaining children in the family household longer and employing their sons, daughters and wives. In this sense, it could be said that they perfected the sweated labour system to meet their own end. With this rapid transformation in the working structure of the Jewish family, it is appropriate that attention is now turned more directly to family and household composition.

Family

The main characteristics of household structure for the four migrant groups are depicted in Tables 7 and 8, for male and female headed households respectively.[71] In the case of male-headed households, the migrant households display a lower proportion of 'nuclear' or 'simple' families (married couple with or without children, and lone parent families) and conversely a higher proportion of extended family groups than the native Bethnal Green households. This is perhaps only to be expected given the findings of Anderson, who for mid-nineteenth-

	1891		1901		1911		1921	
	n.	%	n.	%	n.	%	n.	%
Bethnal Green								
Solitaries	12	1.7	40	3.1	24	2.8	29	3.9
Co-resident kin	6	0.8	16	1.3	23	2.6	21	2.9
Married couple:								
without children	114	15.9	150	11.8	100	11.5	98	13.3
with child(ren)	491	68.3	857	67.3	580	66.8	485	66.0
Lone parent with child(ren)	20	2.8	96	7.5	38	4.4	34	4.6
Extended	67	9.3	105	8.2	83	9.6	56	7.6
Multiple	9	1.3	10	0.8	20	2.3	12	1.6
Total households	719	100.0	1,274	100.0	868	100.0	735	100.0
Within London								
Solitaries	6	1.7	20	4.2	16	3.9	19	4.5
Co-resident kin	1	0.3	5	1.0	7	1.7	4	0.9
Married couple:								
without children	62	17.3	70	14.6	71	17.4	58	13.7
with child(ren)	246	68.5	308	64.3	238	58.5	276	65.2
Lone parent with child(ren)	16	4.5	22	4.6	20	4.9	16	3.8
Extended	26	7.2	49	10.2	52	12.8	43	10.2
Multiple	2	0.6	5	1.0	3	0.7	7	1.7
Total households	359	100.0	479	100.0	407	100.0	423	100.0
Outside London								
Solitaries	7	1.9	26	6.0	16	5.4	8	5.2
Co-resident kin	2	0.5	7	1.6	3	1.0	2	1.3
Married couple:								
without children	62	16.6	81	18.8	53	17.7	34	21.9
with child(ren)	246	66.0	256	59.3	172	57.5	86	55.5
Lone parent with child(ren)	10	2.7	16	3.7	11	3.7	8	5.2
Extended	38	10.2	43	10.0	41	13.7	10	6.5
Multiple	8	2.1	3	0.7	3	1.0	7	4.5
Total households	373	100.0	432	100.0	299	100.0	155	100.0
Eastern Europe								
Solitaries	0	-	8	5.1	10	2.9	5	1.4
Co-resident kin	0	-	1	0.6	1	0.3	0	-
Married couple:								
without children	3	11.1	11	7.1	22	6.3	31	8.8
with child(ren)	18	66.7	110	70.5	268	77.2	281	79.6
Lone parent with child(ren)	5	18.5	7	4.5	3	0.9	12	3.4
Extended	1	3.7	17	10.9	41	11.8	19	5.4
Multiple	0	-	2	1.3	2	0.6	5	1.4
Total households	27	100.0	156	100.0	347	100.0	353	100.0

**Table 7. Household structure by migrant group, male-headed households
1891-1921**

century Preston has emphasised the role of kin in assisting the migration process, especially in terms of helping to provide accommodation for new arrivals to the city and in other times of extreme crisis.[72] Indeed, those migrating from outside of London show a slight tendency towards higher proportions of extended and multiple households than those migrating to Bethnal Green from within London. This group also displays the highest numbers of solitary households. This trend is also mirrored by the situation of female-headed households (Table 8). For these households, those women born outside of London tend to record slightly higher proportions of solitary and extended households than either the London migrants or native Bethnal Green. Despite, the presumed greater numbers of kin available locally for the native Bethnal Green population, it was the migrant households, especially those from outside of London that showed a greater propensity to live with relatives. This is not to say that kinship for the Bethnal Greeners was unimportant, but rather for them kinship ties tended to operate between households rather than within households.

In contrast, the migrant Jewish households present a very different picture. For them the link between migration and non-nuclear household structure is very much broken. Of all the four groups the eastern European households display the most nuclear family structures. This is especially true in 1921 by which date the proportion of male-headed households which were either extended or multiple were less than half of the other two migrant groups and smaller also than the native Bethnal Green population. The number of solitary households are also at very low levels amongst the Jewish population. Clear differences can also be seen in relation to female-headed households. Not only are the overall numbers of female-headed households low *pro rata*–being totally absent in 1891–but also solitary households were comparatively few, as were the presence of extended households.[73] Indeed, multiple households simply did not occur for eastern European female heads of household. For the new Jewish immigrants of East London the nuclear household form dominated.

This finding would appear to be at odds not only with the patterns shown by the other migrant households in this study, but moreover would appear to contradict the expectations of Hajnal's eastern European household formation model and other studies that have shown 'Russian' households to be traditionally dominated by large complex kin-orientated resident groups.[74] It is certainly the case that the tendency toward nuclear family households would have been influenced by the age profile of the eastern European migrants (see Table 3), with older heads showing a greater propensity to form either solitary, extended or multiple households, but it would seem implausible that age structure alone could have accounted for this unexpected difference. In consequence, the comparative situation of household structure requires further investigation.

	1891 n.	1891 %	1901 n.	1901 %	1911 n.	1911 %	1921 n.	1921 %
Bethnal Green								
Solitaries	22	15.6	78	26.7	45	23.6	34	18.9
Co-resident kin	10	7.1	20	6.8	17	8.9	30	16.7
Lone parent with child(ren)	91	64.5	162	55.5	101	52.9	92	51.1
Extended	17	12.1	28	9.6	22	11.5	15	8.3
Multiple	1	0.7	4	1.4	6	3.1	9	5.0
Total households	141	100.0	292	100.0	191	100.0	180	100.0
Within London								
Solitaries	15	18.5	34	25.0	25	28.7	40	37.7
Co-resident kin	3	3.7	8	5.9	9	10.3	10	9.4
Lone parent with child(ren)	54	66.7	81	59.6	42	48.3	45	42.5
Extended	9	11.1	10	7.4	8	9.2	9	8.5
Multiple	0	-	3	2.2	3	3.4	2	1.9
Total households	81	100.0	136	100.0	87	100.0	106	100.0
Outside London								
Solitaries	16	21.9	26	25.7	16	22.2	21	40.4
Co-resident kin	4	5.5	7	6.9	5	6.9	4	7.7
Lone parent with child(ren)	46	63.0	55	54.5	39	54.2	19	36.5
Extended	6	8.2	11	10.9	11	15.3	7	13.5
Multiple	1	1.4	2	2.0	1	1.4	1	1.9
Total households	73	100.0	101	100.0	72	100.0	52	100.0
Eastern Europe								
Solitaries	0	-	3	15.8	4	14.3	15	22.7
Co-resident kin	0	-	1	5.3	1	3.6	1	1.5
Lone parent with child(ren)	0	-	13	68.4	20	71.4	46	69.7
Extended	0	-	2	10.5	3	10.7	4	6.1
Multiple	0	-	0	-	0	-	0	-
Total households	0	-	19	100.0	28	100.0	66	100.0

Table 8. Household structure by migrant group, female-headed households 1891-1921

The information on household structures provided in Tables 7 and 8 relates only to household heads and their co-resident kin. In this regard it is important to realise that households in this period were augmented by the presence of both servants and inmates attached to the main resident group of the household head.[75] To address this issue Figures 7 through to 15 show in diagrammatic form the relationship of all individuals to head of households by age and gender for the four migrant populations in 1901, while Figures 16 through to 23 display the same for 1921. In these figures, relationship to head of household is classified simply into one of five categories: never-married offspring (offsp), head or spouse of head (headsp), co-residing relative (relat), servant (servt) or inmate (inmate).[76] Comparison of the figures reveal some interesting differences between the four migrants groups. Turning first to the situation of males in 1901, there are a number of characteristics that persist overtime and a number that change. Unsurprisingly, those UK migrants born outside of London show the highest level of boarding and lodging (collectively termed inmates) in both years. However, although this peaks at some 20 per cent in the age group 21–25 in 1901 and 16 per cent in the age group 26–30 in 1921, the later census year reveals a situation in which boarding and lodging had become a more common feature over the whole course of the life cycle, especially for those over 45 of whom some 7-8 per cent lived as inmates. This migrant group also displays relatively large proportions residing in the households of kin as relatives, confirming the greater tendency toward extended type households as noted above. In 1901 this feature is particularly marked for the 21–25 and 26–30 age groups (10 and 7 per cent respectively), while in 1921 the number living as relatives was both higher and peaked later (at 21 per cent in the age group 26–30), with higher proportions in the later stages of the life cycle also. The higher numbers of inmates and kin aged in their twenties in the case of these migrants would appear to be a feature of their migrant status, and shows some support for Anderson's view that migrants to urban areas were often assisted by kin, especially at the time of arrival.[77] However, it also suggests that the timing of migration was perhaps occurring slightly later, up to five years later, in 1921 compared to 1901. This pattern of later migration is also displayed by those migrating within London, for whom the proportions living as relatives peaked at 15 per cent in 1901 in the age group 21–25 and 13 per cent in the age group 26–30 in 1921. Yet unlike those males migrating from outside London the proportions living as inmates were comparatively low. The most dramatic changes, however, occurred in the case of those from eastern Europe. In 1901 a large proportion of Jewish immigrants, unsurprisingly, lived as inmates, particularly between the ages of 16 and 30, with some 20 to 30 per cent of this age residing as boarders or lodgers. Yet by 1921 the residential arrangements of the Jews had been transformed. Hardly any lived as inmates, with nearly all those of eastern European origin living within simple 'nuclear' families as either unmarried sons or heads of their own household. Turning to the native Bethnal Green born, it is interesting to note that the pattern living with kin was unlike any of the other three migrant groups. Comparatively, the co-residing kin were more important over the whole course of the life cycle, and increased in importance between 1901 and 1921. Thus, for the Bethnal Green natives kinship was increasingly being used to help support both young and old, possibly pointing to increased local pressures on housing in a time of economic hardship. Lastly, the native Bethnal Green males also display a change over time that effected all four groups to a greater of lesser extent. In parallel with the timing of migration being delayed between 1901 and 1921, it was also the case that children were staying in the parental home longer and consequently forming independent households later. For those born in Bethnal Green the number of males living in the parental home as unmarried sons rose from 45 to 60 per cent and from 17 to 23 per cent for the two age groups 21–25 and 26–30 between 1901 and 1921. Likewise, the proportions of heads of household in these two age groups decreased from 44 to 29 and from 73 to 64 per cent, respectively, between 1901 and 1921. Similar patterns can also be seen for the London-born male migrants and those born outside of London, however, the most dramatic transition in this regard occurred in the case of the Jewish immigrants. Details of how the Jewish 'working family' was transformed during this period have already been discussed, and in line with these changes it is important to note that the proportions of unmarried sons living in the parental home in the three age groups 16–20, 21–25 and 26–30 rose from 55, 13 and 5 per cent to 100, 92 and 47 per cent respectively between 1901 and 1921. Likewise the proportions of male heads of household in these three age groups fell from 5, 48 and 62 per cent to just 0, 5 and 50 per cent over the course of the twenty years between the two censuses. The Jewish immigrants not only rapidly transformed

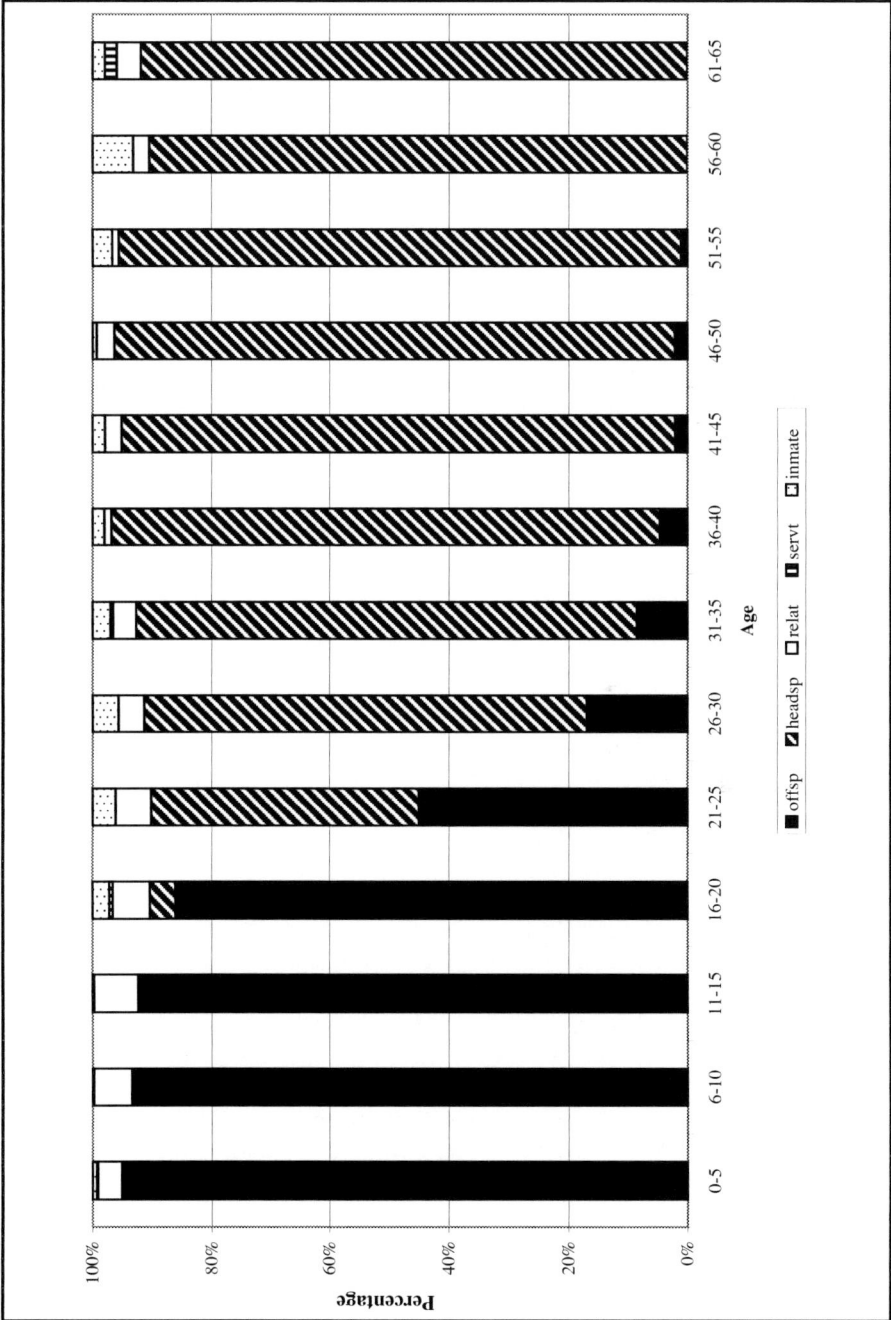

Figure 7. Relationship to household head by age. Bethnal Green born males, 1901

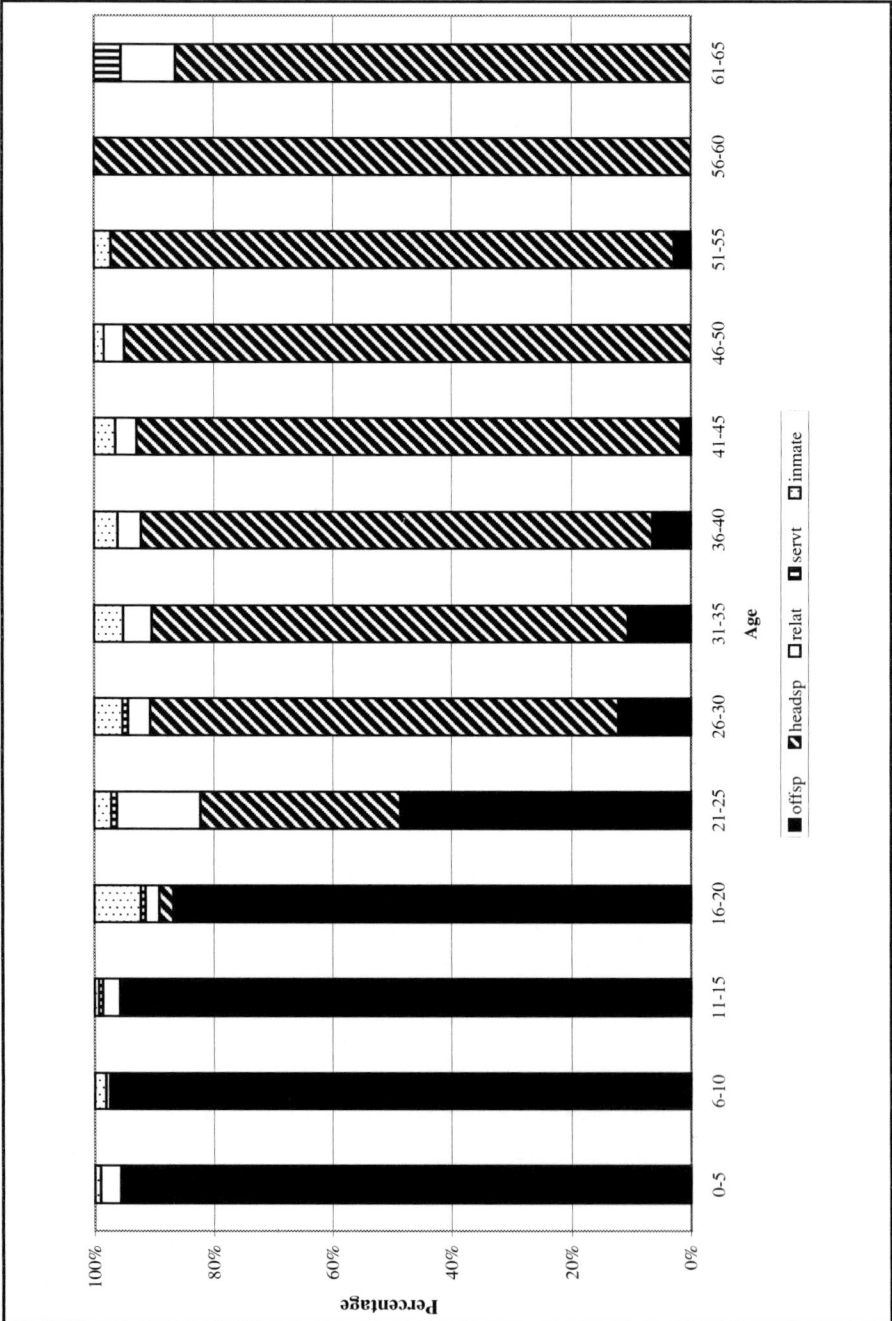

Figure 8. Relationship to household head by age. London-born males, 1901

Legend: offsp | headsp | relat | servt | inmate

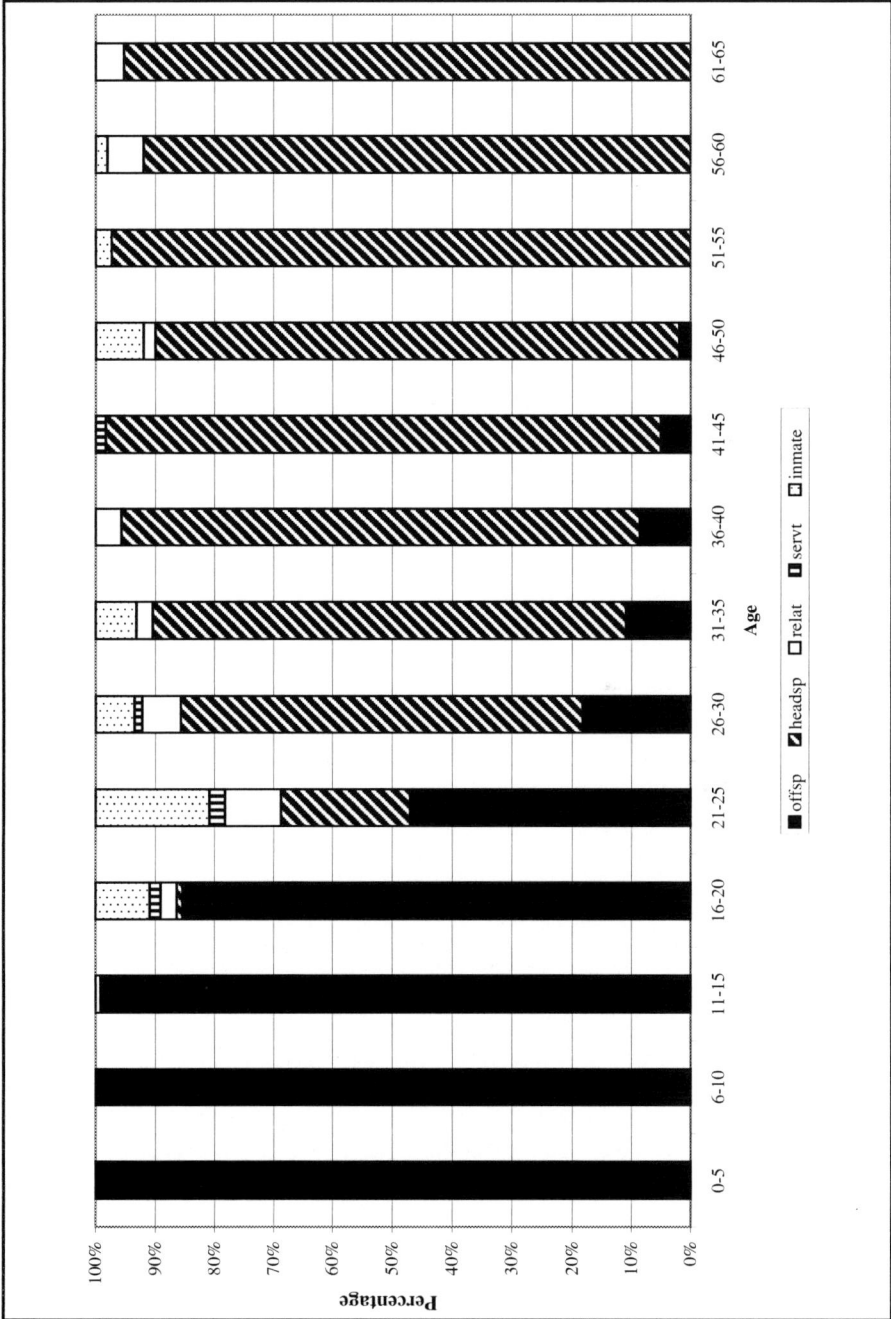

Figure 9. Relationship to household head by age. Male migrants, 1901

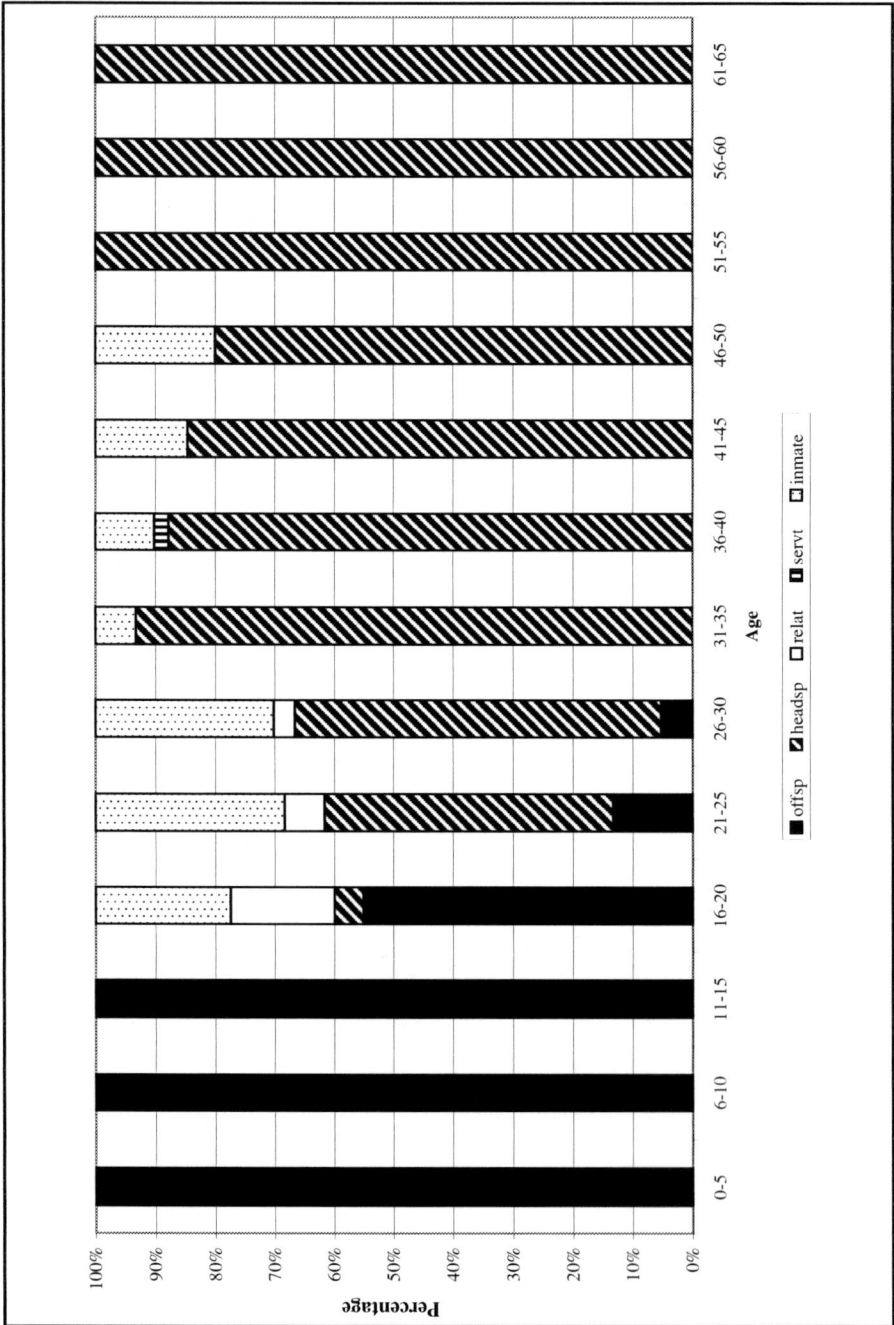

Figure 10. Relationship to household head by age. Eastern european born males, 1901

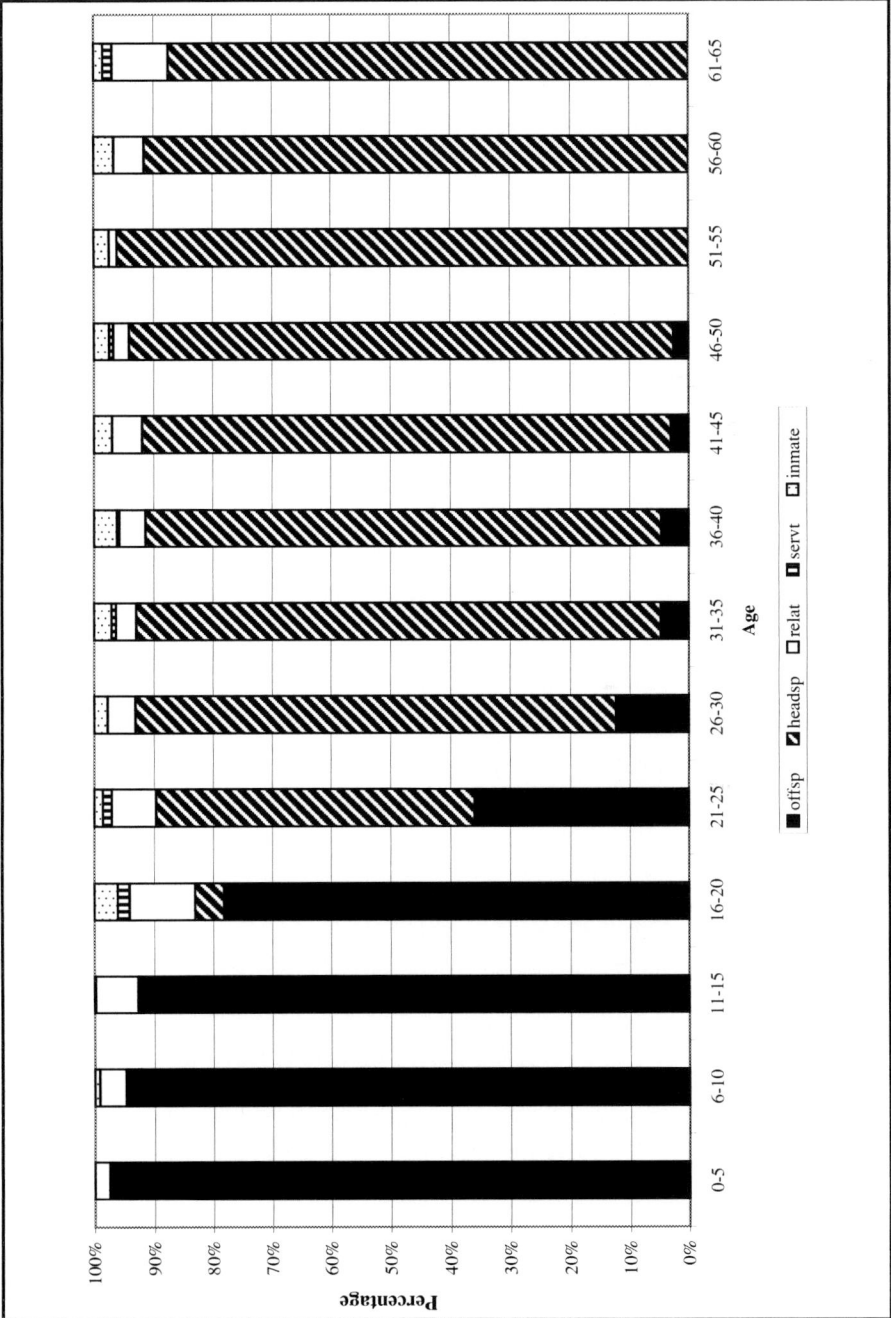

Figure 11. Relationship to household head by age. Bethnal Green born females, 1901

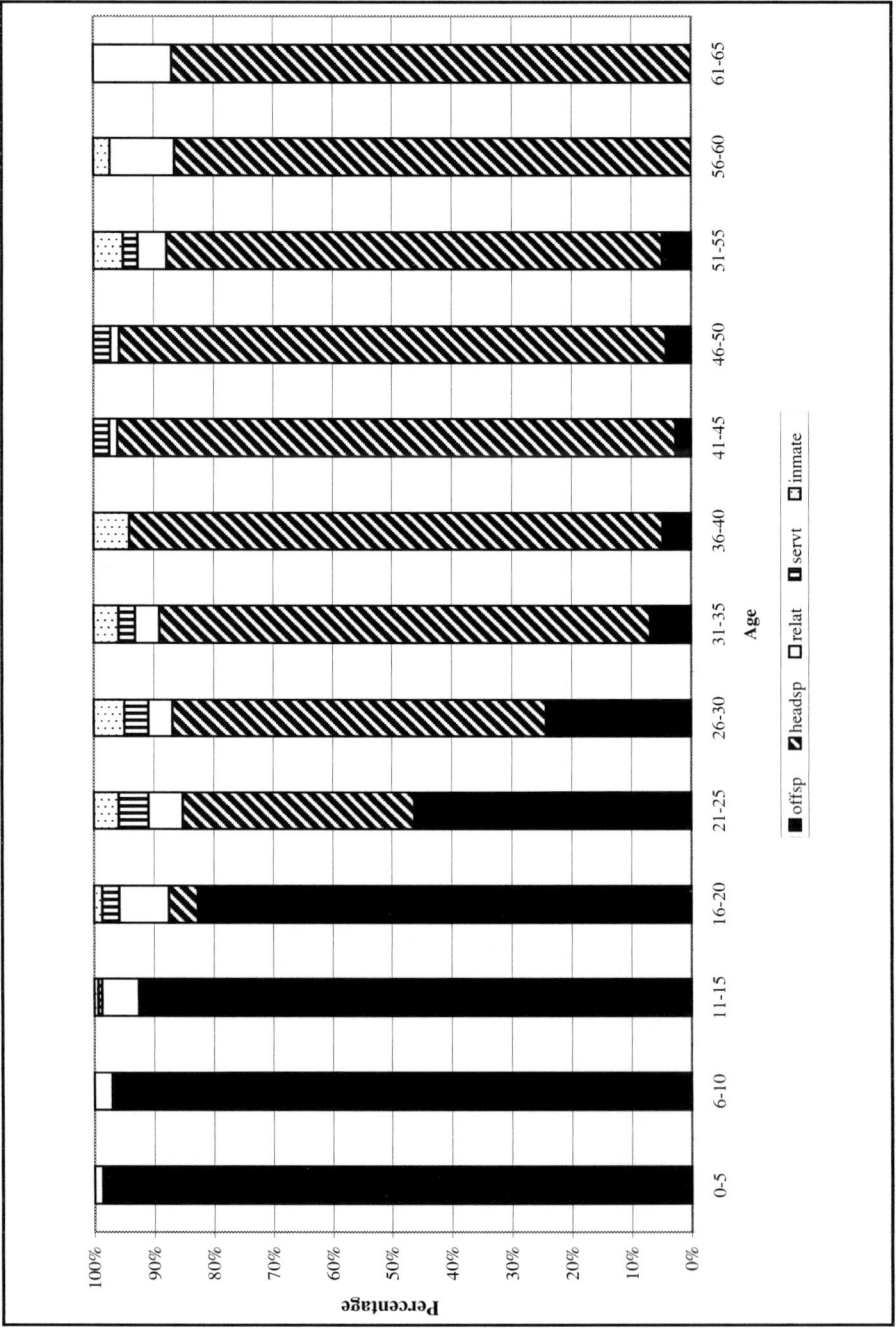

Figure 12. Relationship to household head by age. London-born females, 1901

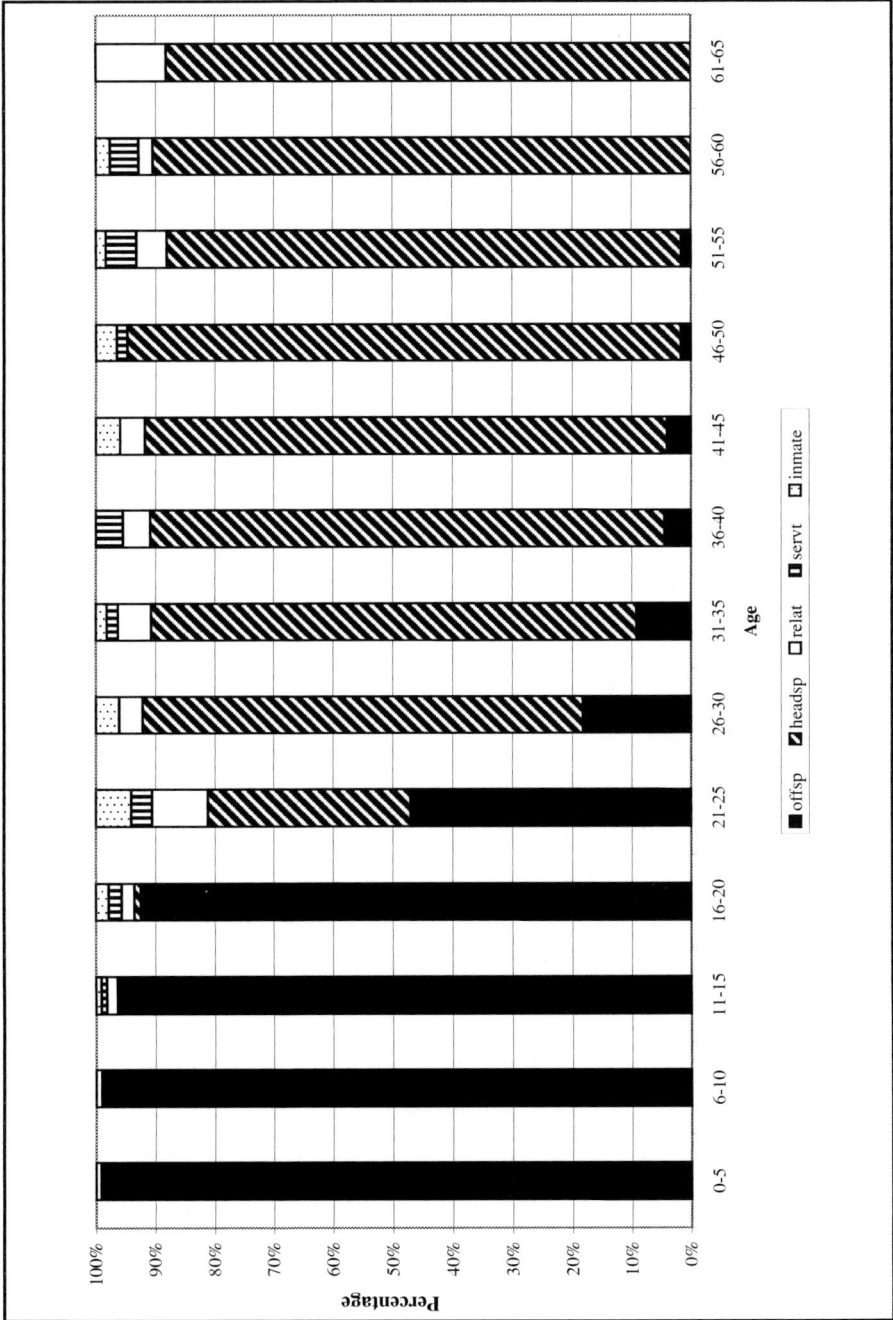

Figure 13. Relationship to household head by age. Female migrants, 1901

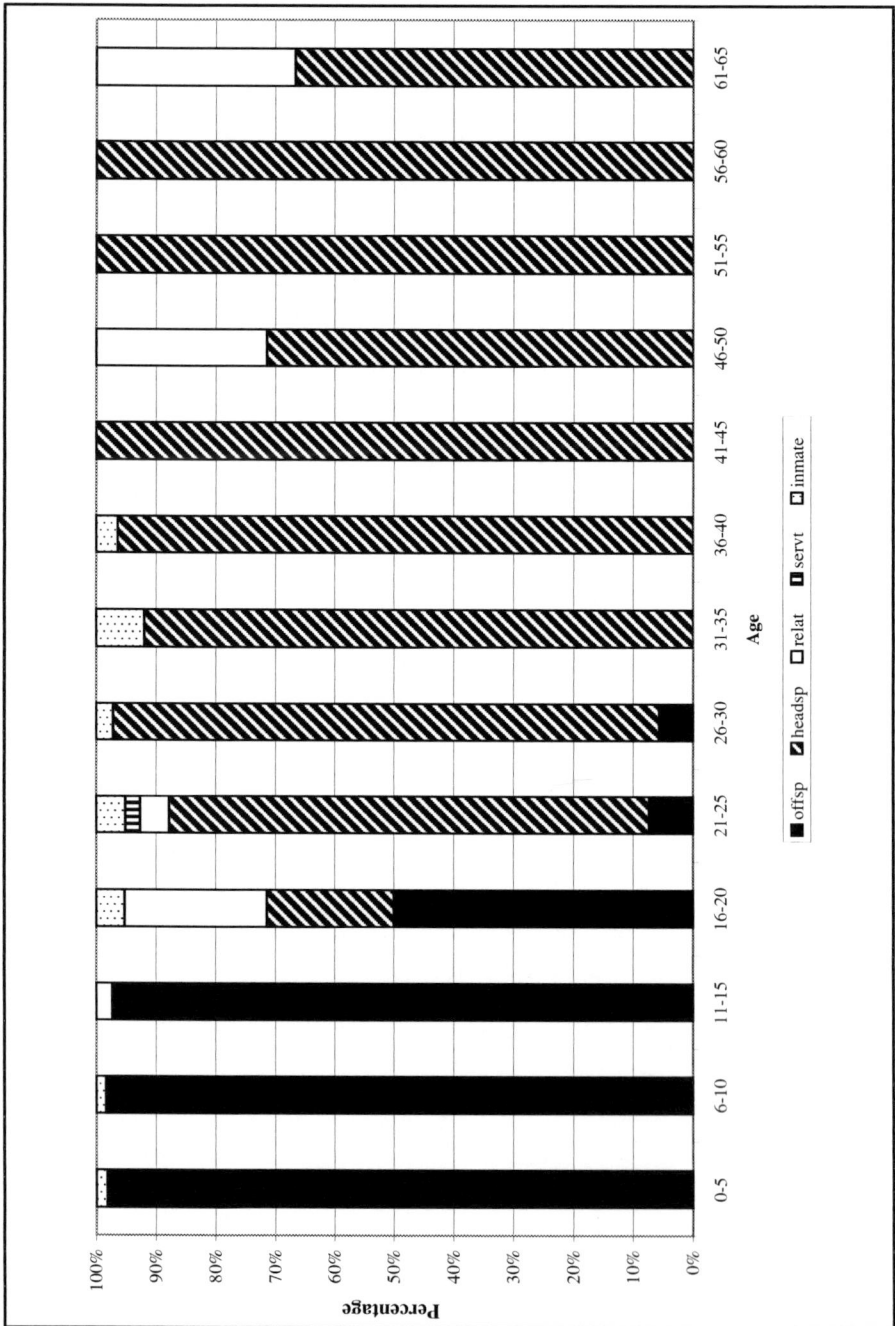

Figure 14. Relationship to household head by age. Eastern european born females, 1921

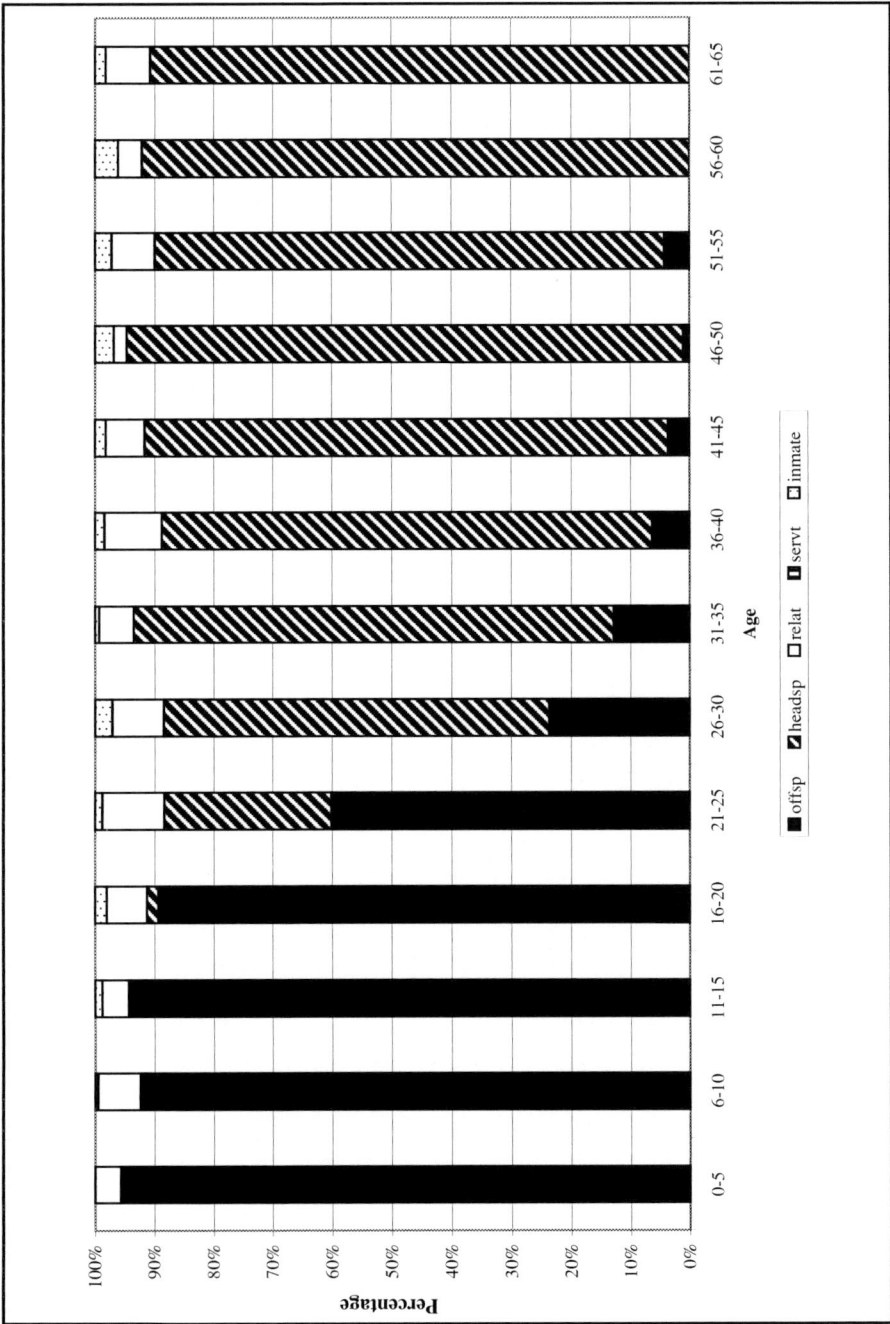

Figure 15. Relationship to household head by age. Bethnal Green born males, 1921

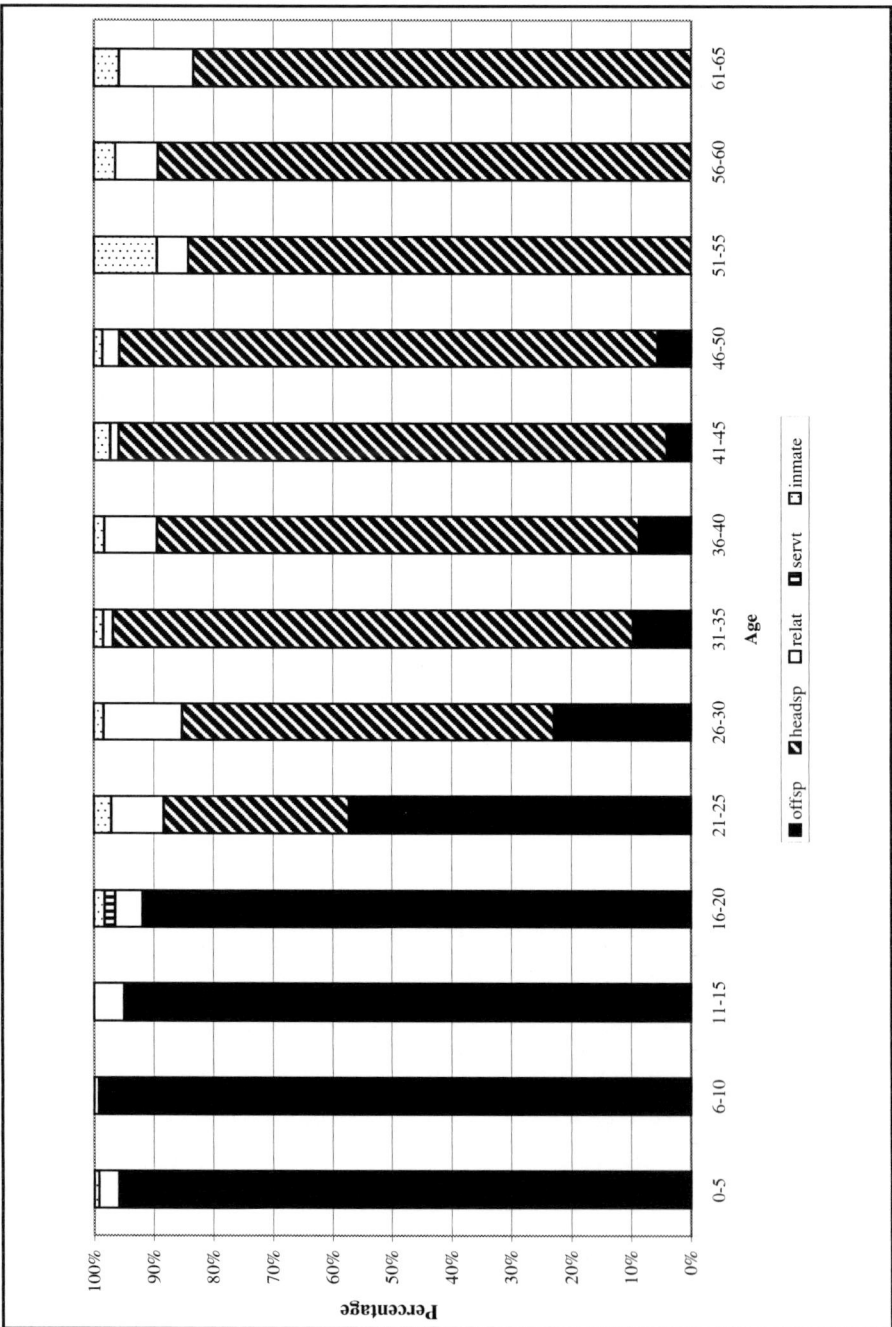

Figure 16. Relationship to household head by age. London-born males, 1921

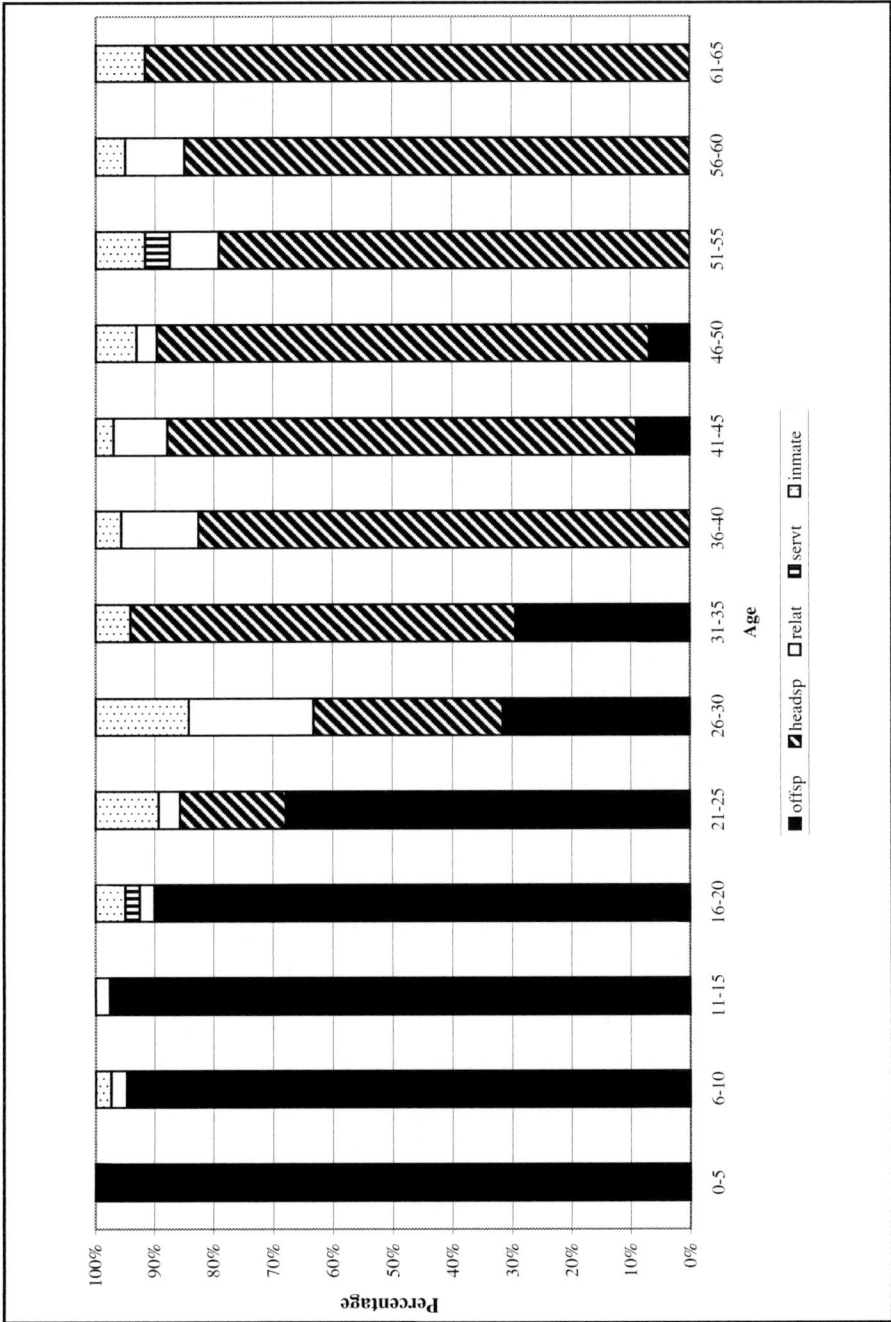

Figure 17. Relationship to household head by age. Male migrants, 1901

Legend: ■ offsp ▨ headsp □ relat ▥ servt ▱ inmate

Age

Percentage

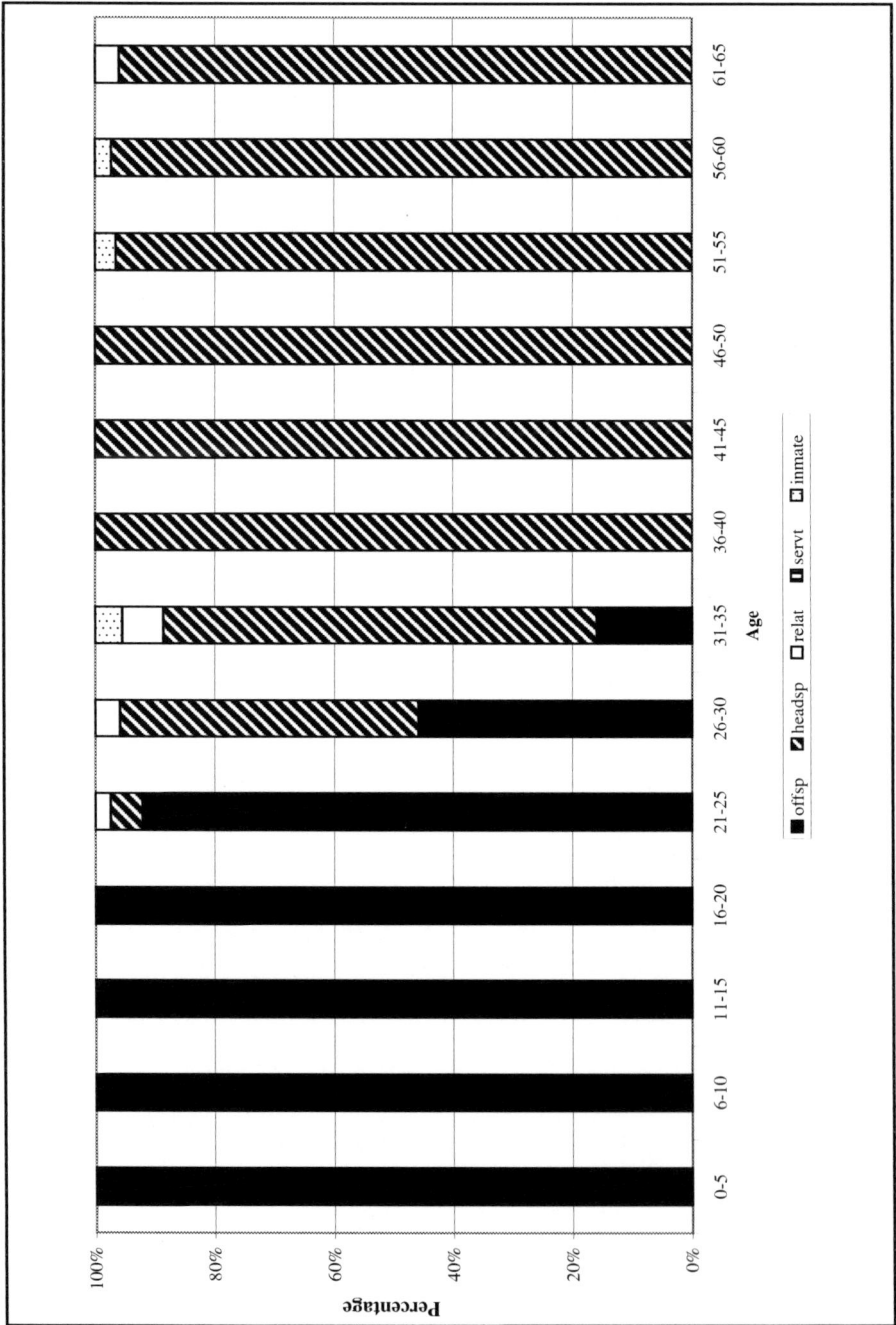

Figure 18. Relationship to household head by age. Eastern european born males, 1921

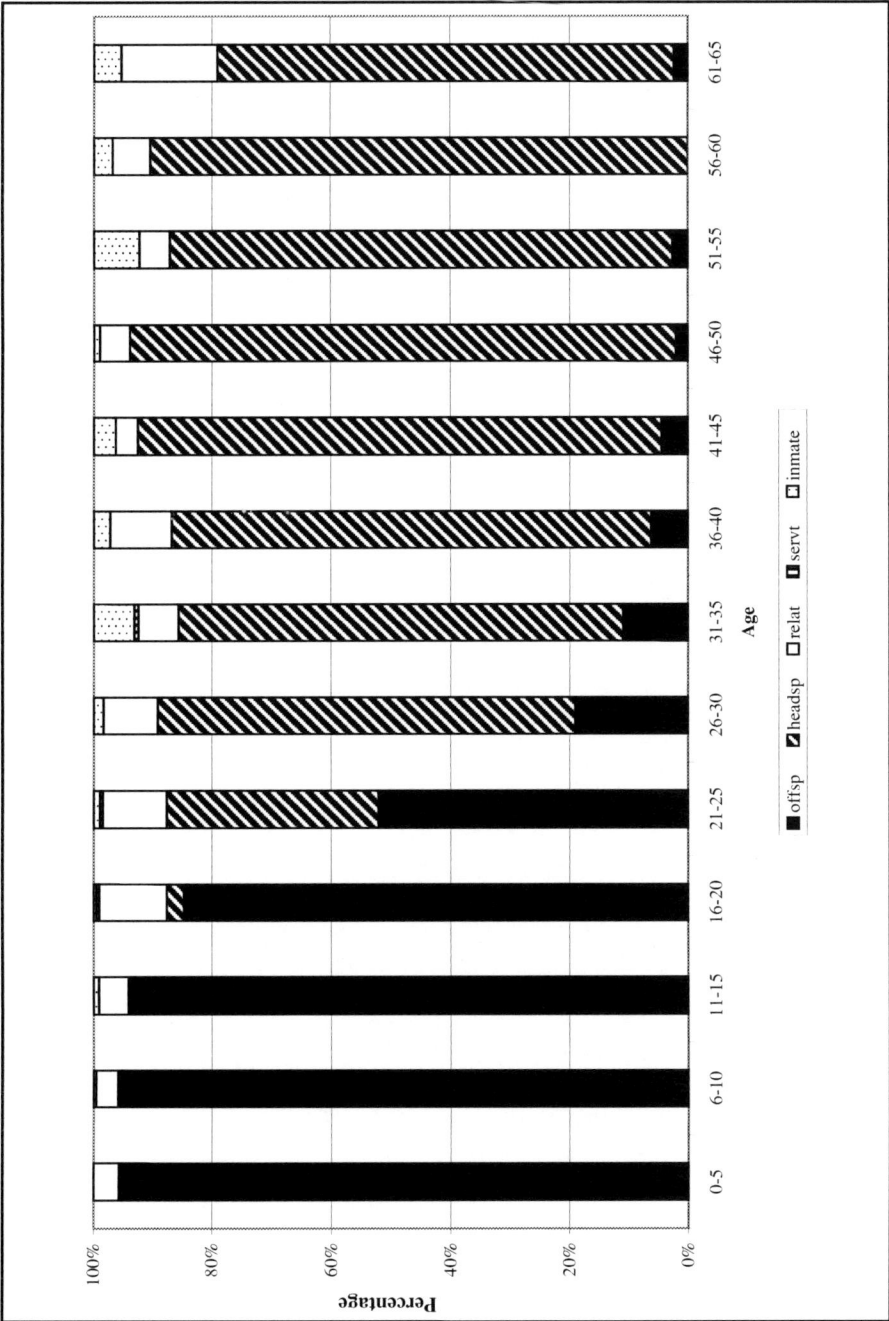

Figure 19. Relationship to household head by age. Bethnal Green born males, 1921

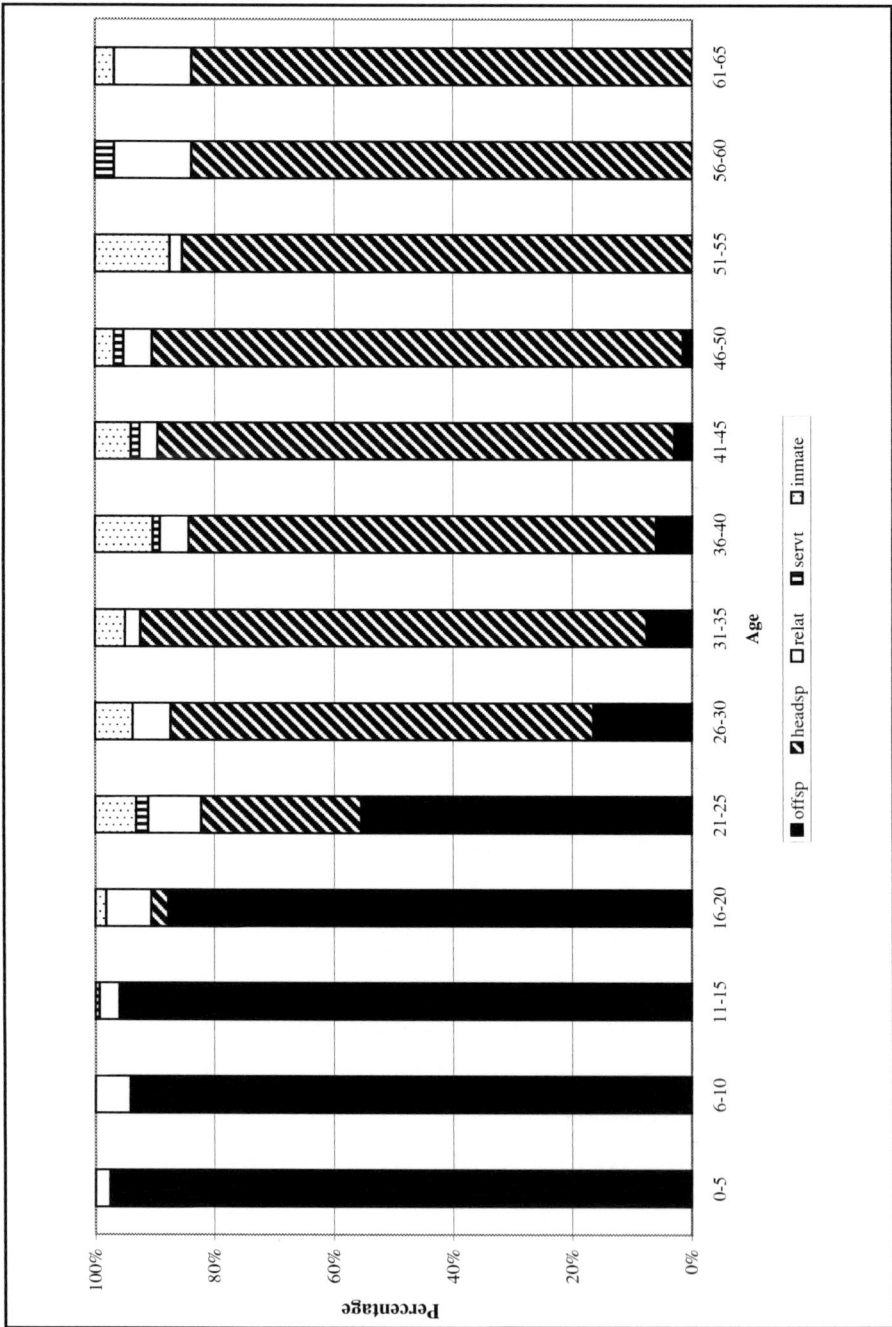

Figure 20. Relationship to household head by age. London-born males, 1921

Legend: ■ offsp ▨ headsp ☐ relat ■ servt ☐ inmate

Age (x-axis): 0-5, 6-10, 11-15, 16-20, 21-25, 26-30, 31-35, 36-40, 41-45, 46-50, 51-55, 56-60, 61-65

Percentage (y-axis): 0%, 20%, 40%, 60%, 80%, 100%

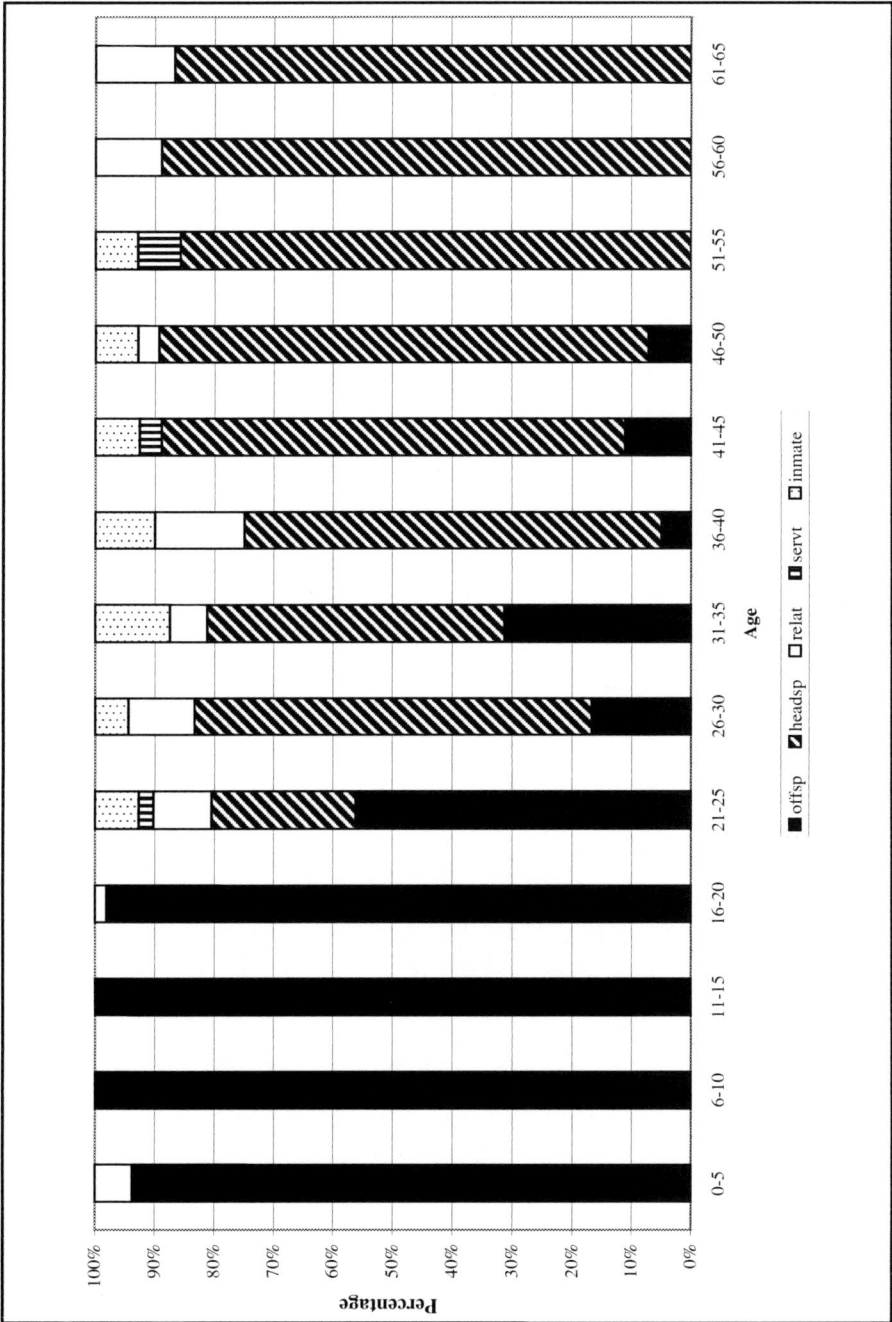

Figure 21. Relationship to household head by age. Male migrants, 1901

Legend: ■ offsp ▨ headsp □ relat ▤ servt □ inmate

X-axis (Age): 0-5, 6-10, 11-15, 16-20, 21-25, 26-30, 31-35, 36-40, 41-45, 46-50, 51-55, 56-60, 61-65

Y-axis (Percentage): 0%, 10%, 20%, 30%, 40%, 50%, 60%, 70%, 80%, 90%, 100%

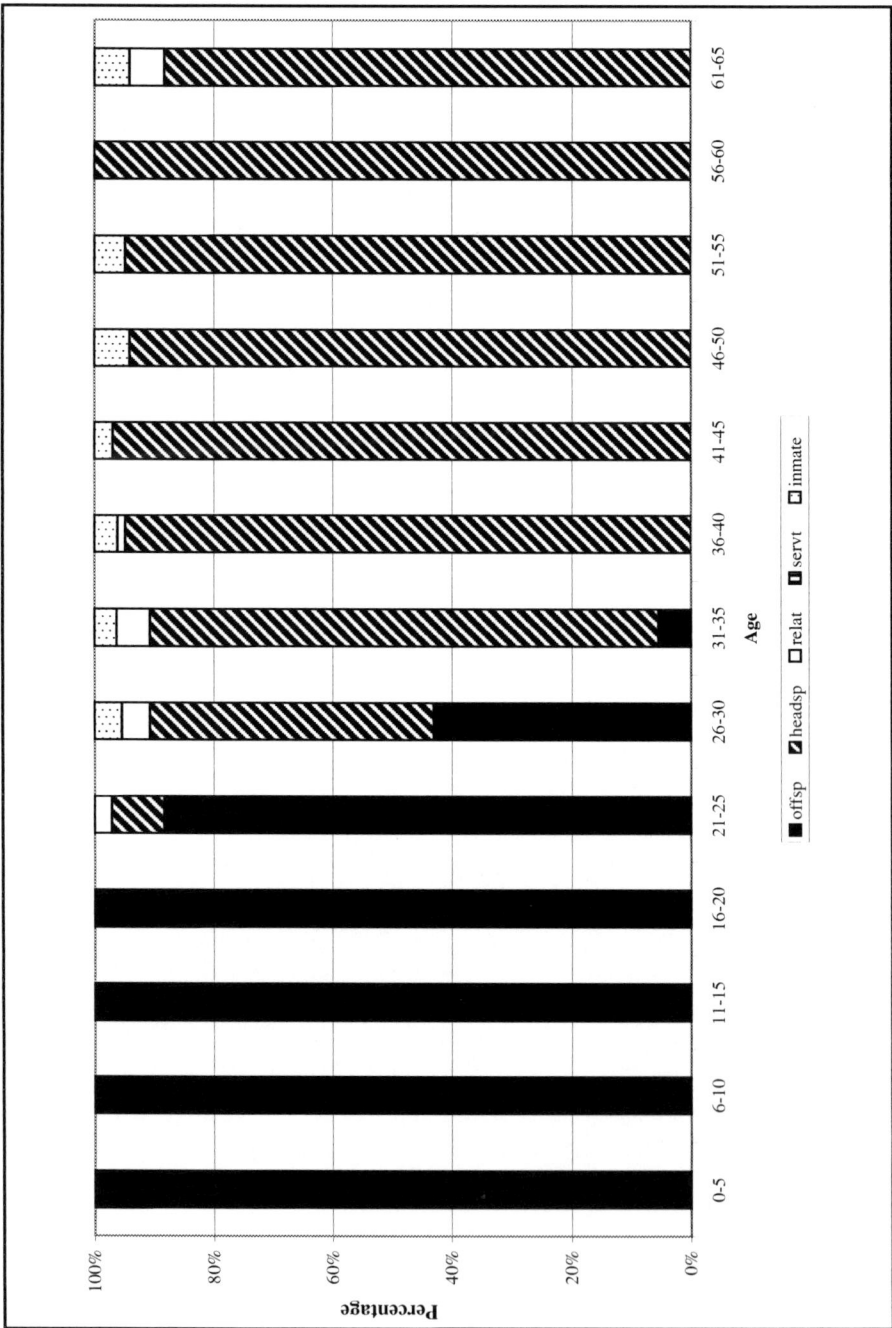

Figure 22. Relationship to household head by age. Eastern european born males, 1921

their familial working arrangements, but also their demographic and household formation patterns. Despite having in 1901 a pattern of relatively early marriage[78] and early attainment of headship, by 1921 the Jews were delaying marriage and household formation, experiencing later marriage than even the native born of Bethnal Green.

Many of the residential arrangements just discussed for males in 1901 and 1921 were mirrored by females. However, there were also some important differences. Living as co-resident domestic servants was one obvious and important difference. Bethnal Green was home to few female servants, but those that were servants tended to be migrants from within London or from outside of London. For these two migrant groups living as co-resident kin was also comparatively important, but unlike their male counterparts migrant females lived with relatives at older ages (aged 56 and over), a tendency that increased over time. It may be that these elderly women moved into Bethnal Green late in life to reside with relatives following the death of their own spouse or some similar familial crisis. As with males, the increased tendency to live with kin throughout the life cycle was also displayed by the native born females of Bethnal Green. Equally, the tendency toward remaining in the parental home longer and forming independent households later was displayed by all group, but especially the native Bethnal Green born and the immigrants from eastern Europe. As with males, the pattern of household formation amongst young Jewish women was rapidly and dramatically transformed. Of those aged between 21–25 and 26–30, in 1901, 8 and 6 per cent were unmarried daughters living with their parents, while 80 and 91 per cent were spouses, respectively. By 1921, 89 and 43 per cent were still living at home as daughters, and just 10 and 26 per cent, respectively were spouses. This transformation in family composition amongst the Jewish immigrants is all the more striking when viewed in relation to the traditional notion of eastern European families marrying early and co-residing in large complex family groups, as discussed at the beginning of this chapter. Either this shows a remarkable propensity for the Jews to assimilate into a new culture, or questions the extent to which the household composition and structure of eastern European Jewish families were similar to the non-Jewish population.

Conclusion

This chapter has examined the employment patterns and living arrangements of four groups within the labour force of Bethnal Green at the end of the nineteenth and beginning of the twentieth centuries. Although differences between the native-born population and the various migrant groups can be observed, there is little general support for the theory of urban degeneration. The labour force experience of migrants into Bethnal Green clearly varied and migrants could not be seen as being in a universally favoured position in comparison to the non-migrant local born population. The migration experience of the Jewish immigrants from eastern Europe was also fundamentally different from migrants both moving into the area from other parts of London and from outside of London. The eastern European immigrants appeared not to adopt familial and household structures typical of the countries they left behind them, but rather rapidly transformed their demographic behaviour and patterns of household formation to create stereotypical 'nuclear' families. Whether this transformation was driven by economic needs, constraints in housing accommodation[79] or a desire to assimilate themselves into English society it is impossible to say. However, in as much that their family structures in 1921 resembled those of late twentieth-century Britain more closely than their newly-found Bethnal Green neighbours, they had done exactly what the middle class Jewish élite of London had wanted them to do—become English.

Acknowledgements

Census data contained in this paper are reproduced with the permission of the Controller of Her Majesty's Stationery Office. Crown Copyright.

I am grateful to Alice Reid of the Cambridge Group for the History of Population and Social Structure for running some of the initial tabulations on the 1891 to 1921 census material, and to Julie Gammon who assisted in the classification of birthplaces and Nick Hewes who prepared some of the figures. I am also indebted to Matthew Woollard who provided helpful comments on an earlier version of this paper.

NOTES

[1]   E. G. Ravenstein, 'The laws of migration', *Journal of the Statistical Society*, 48 (1885), 167–227 and E. G. Ravenstein, 'The laws of migration', *Journal of the Royal Statistical Society*, 52 (1889), 214–301; E. S. Lee, 'A theory of migration', *Demography*, 3 (1966), 47–57. See also A. Redford, *Labour migration in England, 1800–1850* (London, 1976) and the more recent work of C. Pooley and J. Turnball, *Migration and mobility in Britain since the eighteenth century* (London, 1998) which from different perspectives both emphasise the links between migration and economic development. A useful overview of the work of Ravenstein and the applicability of his 'laws of migration' is given in D. B. Grigg, 'E. G. Ravenstein and the laws of migration', *Journal of Historical Geography* 3 (1977), 41–54.

[2]   Particularly influential are the economic models developed by Todaro. See J. R. Harris and M. P. Todaro, 'Migration, unemployment and development: a two sector analysis', *American Economic Review*, 60 (1970), 126–42 and M. P. Todaro, 'A model of labor, migration and urban unemployment in less developed countries', *American Economic Review*, 59 (1969), 138–48.

[3]   C. Booth, ed., *Life and labour in London*, series 1 & 2, 9 volumes, series 3, 7 volumes plus 'final volume' (London, 1892–1902).

[4]   H. Llewellyn Smith, 'The influx of population', in Booth, ed., *Life and labour*, III (London, 1892), 58–111. Cited here at 110–111.

[5]   G. Stedman Jones, *Outcast London* (London, 1976).

[6]   T. J. Hatton and R. E. Bailey, 'Natives and migrants in the London labour market 1929–31', paper delivered to the CEPR conference on Marginal labour markets in metropolitan areas, Dublin, 1999. Findings from the New Survey of London Life and Labour are reported in the multi-authored volumes *New Survey* published between 1930–4.

[7]   J. Hajnal, 'European marriage patterns in perspective', in D. V. Glass and D. E. C. Eversley, eds, *Population in history: essays in historical demography* (London, 1965), 101–143. See also J Hajnal, 'Two kinds of preindustrial household formation system', *Population and Development Review*, 8 (1982), 449–494. Reprinted in R. Wall, J. Robin and P. Laslett, eds, *Family forms in historic Europe* (Cambridge, 1983), 65–104; P. Laslett, 'Family and household as work group and kin group: areas of traditional Europe compared', in R. Wall, J. Robin and P. Laslett, eds, *Family forms in historic Europe* (Cambridge, 1983), 513–63; P. Laslett, 'The institution of service', *Local Population Studies*, 40 (1987), 55–60 and R. M. Smith, 'Fertility, economy and household formation in England over three centuries', *Population and Development Review*, 7 (1981), 595–622 all of which further develop the original model proposed by Hajnal.

[8]   G. Alter, 'New perspectives on European marriage in the nineteenth century', *Journal of Family History*, 16:1 (1991), 1–5. Cited here at p.1. For criticism of Hajnal's model, especially in relation to its applicability to southern Europe see, P. P. Viazzo, 'What's distinctive about the Mediterranean? Thirty years of research on household and family in Italy', paper delivered at 'Household and Family in Past Time' conference, Palma, University of the Balearics, September 8–11, 1999; R. Rowland, 'Household and family in the Iberian peninsula', paper delivered at

'Household and Family in Past Time' conference, Palma, University of the Balearics, September 8–11, 1999; M. Todorova, 'Situating the family of Ottoman Bulgaria within the European pattern', *Journal of Family History*, 1:4 (1996), 443–459; V. Hionidou, 'Nuptiality patterns and household structure on the Greek island of Mykonos, 1849–1959', *Journal of Family History*, 20:1 (1995), 67–102.

[9]   M. Young and P. Willmott, *Family and kinship in East London* (London, 1957).

[10]   Young and Willmott, *Family and kinship*, 85.

[11]   Young and Willmott, *Family and kinship*, 84.

[12]   J. H. Robb, *Working class anti-semite* (London, 1954).

[13]   C. Booth, 'Statistics of poverty', in Booth, ed., *Life and labour*, II (London, 1892), 18–39, here at p.31. This measure is taking districts with a total population of around 100,000. The district with the highest level of poverty was Southwark/Bermondsey with 60 per cent of the population in poverty. The next was Greenwich with 54 per cent.

[14]   A. Morrison, *A child of the Jago* (London, 1969). This edition includes a useful 'Biographical study' of Morrison by P. J. Keating.

[15]   See Keating, 'Biographical study'.

[16]   J. White, *Rothschild buildings. Life in an East End tenement block 1887–1920* (London, 1980), 24–6.

[17]   Artizans' and Labourers' Dwellings Improvement Act (38 & 39 Vict., cap. xxxvi) [1875].

[18]   See for example, H. J. Dyos and D. A. Reeder, 'Slums and suburbs', in H. J. Dyos and M. Woolf, eds, *The Victorian city: images and realities* (London, 1973), 359–386.

[19]   J. Greenwood, *In strange company* (London, 1883), 158. Cited in White, *Rothschild buildings*, 6.

[20]   A clear example of this process is provided by White, *Rothschild buildings*, 9–30. In Morrison's *Jago* many inhabitants refuse to move out for lack of anywhere else to go.

[21]   C. Booth, *Life and labour*, II (series 3) (London, 1902), 1.

[22]   For accounts of the pogroms in Russia and the resulting Jewish migration see H. Pollins, *Economic history of the Jews in England* (London, 1982); L. Gartner, *The Jewish immigrant in England, 1870–1914* (London, 1973, second edition); and the various contributions to D. Berger, ed., *The legacy of Jewish migration: 1881 and its impact* (London, 1983).

[23]   Pollins, *Economic history*, 132.

[24]   D. Feldman, *Englishmen and Jews: social relations and political culture, 1840–1914* (London, 1994), 148. However, Feldman also argues that the emigration of Jews from Russia was as much the result of demographic and economic pressures, as it was political. Feldman, *Englishmen and Jews*, 148–55.

[25]   *Select Committee on the Sweating system*, BPP 1888 XX, q.1,000.

[26]   By the mid-nineteenth century there were some 12,000–13,000 Jews in London. This number rose to about 30,000 before the pogroms of 1882. See V. D. Lipman, *Social History of the Jews in England, 1850–1950* (London, 1954), 26–8.

[27]   H. Pollins, *Hopeful travellers: Jewish migrants and settlers in nineteenth century Britain*, London Museum of Jewish Life, Research Papers, 2 (1991).

28   See, for example, J. Jacobs, *Studies in Jewish statistics, social vital, and anthropometric* (London, 1891), 18–21. A useful guide to sources for the study of immigration into the UK is provided by R. Kershaw and M. Pearsall, *Immigrants and aliens. A guide to sources on UK immigration and citizenship*, Public Record Office Readers' Guide No. 22 (Kew, 2000).

29   Pollins, *Economic history*, 132.

30   The 1891, 1901 and 1911 censuses of England and Wales enumerated, respectively, 45,074, 82,844 and 103,244 Russians and Russian Poles living in England and Wales. Of these, 59.3, 64.6 and 61.1 per cent, respectively, were enumerated in London. See, Feldman, *Englishmen and Jews*, Table 3, 157.

31   Beatrice Potter comments that the association with London's East End resulted from Spanish and Portuguese Jews settling in Houndsditch from the seventeenth century being permitted to establish a synagogue (the first in England) just outside the eastern boundary of the City, and also being allocated a field in the Mile End for a burial ground. B. Potter, 'The Jewish Community (East London)', in Booth, ed., *Life and labour*, III (London, 1892), 166–92. Cited here at p.166. It is interesting to note that Jews have traditionally tended to favour urban centres rather than rural locations. In some cases this is due to legal restrictions, as was the case in Russia where in 1897 50.5 per cent of the Jewish population lived in urban areas compared to 11.8 per cent of the non-Jewish population, in others occupational. See A. Ruppin, *The Jews of to-day* (London, 1913), 98–105. Jacobs also notes the importance of the Jewish religion itself as a factor influencing the concentration of Jews within a single area. 'Throughout the Diaspora, Jews have been prevented from holding land, and have, therefore, had no inducement to settle in the country, and in many places they were obliged to dwell within fixed limits, Judengassen, Ghetti, or Jewries. Besides this, their religious enactments only permit the sacred functions of public worship to be performed in the presence of ten males above the age of fifteen, the minimum for a congregation. This involves that at least forty souls should dwell within accessible distance'. Jacobs, *Jewish statistics*, 22–3.

32   Feldman, *Englishmen and Jews*, 168.

33   Aliens Act (5 Edw. VII c.13), 1905.

34   For a discussion of the political background and context of the 1905 Aliens Act see D. Feldman, 'The importance of being English. Jewish immigration and the decay of liberal England', in D. Feldman and G. Stedman Jones, eds, *Metropolis– London. Histories and representations since 1800* (London, 1989), 56–84. For an outline of legislation governing immigration into Britain see, Kershaw and Pearsall, *Immigrants and aliens*, 7–10.

35   The middle-class and upper middle-class Jewish community in nineteenth-century London is examined in T. M. Endelman, 'Communal solidarity among the Jewish elite of Victorian London', *Victorian Studies*, 23 (1985), 491–526.

36   Feldman, 'Importance of being English', 62–3.

37   See, for example, V. D. Lipman, *A century of social service, 1859–1959: the Jewish Board of Guardians* (London, 1959), 94–102, and Feldman, 'Importance of being English', 64–6.

38   Lipman, *Century of social service*, 94. It is important to note that this was voluntary, not forced repatriation. However, the figure of '50,000' has been questioned by Pollins, who points out that this figure is based on some 17,500 'cases' rather than individuals. See Pollins, *Hopeful travellers*, 42.

39 For details see White, *Rothschild buildings*, 17–20.

40 See Feldman, *Englishmen and Jews*.

41 For a detailed discussion of the opposition movements against the Jewish immigration and the passage to the passing of the 1905 Aliens Act see Feldman, 'The importance of being English'.

42 Cited in Feldman, 'The importance of being English', 70–1. However, with regard to the increased level of rates it should be noted that all of London Borough's were experiencing sharp rises in the levels of rates at the end of the nineteenth century.

43 *Royal Commission on Alien Immigration*, BPP 1903.

44 Kershaw and Pearsall, *Immigrants and aliens*, 17.

45 *Fifth Annual Report of the HM Inspector under the Aliens Act*, BPP 1911, X, 35. Cited in Feldman, 'The importance of being English', 76.

46 For a history of the census and its application see E. Higgs, *A clearer sense of the census. The Victorian censuses and historical research* (London, 1996).

47 Details of the census enumerators' books are provided in the various chapters to D. Mills and K. Schürer, eds, *Local communities in the Victorian census enumerators' books* (Oxford, 1996). See also E. A. Wrigley, ed., *Nineteenth-century society: essays in the use of quantitative methods for the study of social history* (Cambridge, 1972) and R. Lawton, ed., *The census and social structure: an interpretative guide to the nineteenth century censuses for England and Wales* (London, 1978).

48 The Central Statistical Office (CSO) and the Office of Population Censuses and Surveys (OPCS) merged to form the Office for National Statistics (ONS) in 1 April 1996.

49 The data were made available with the assistance of an award from the ESRC (award G00232261). For further details of these data see E. Garrett, A. Reid, K. Schürer and S. Srezter, *Changing family size in England and Wales, 1891–1911* (Cambridge, forthcoming, 2001).

50 Further details of each of the locales within the selection are given in E. Garrett *et al., Changing family size*, chapter 2, section 3.

51 A. L. Bowley, 'Area and population', in H. Llewellyn Smith, ed., *The new survey of London life and labour*, volume I (London, 1930), 58–83. Cited here at 74.

52 See J. Hicks and G. Allen, 'Census (Amendment) Bill [HL] Bill 100 of 1999–2000', House of Commons Library research paper 00/42 (2000). It is, however, the case that a separate voluntary enumeration of religious worship was conducted in conjunction with the 1851 census. See C.D. Field, 'The 1851 religious census of Great Britain: a bibliographical guide for the local and regional historian', *The Local Historian*, 27 (1997), 194–217.

53 See, for example S. Waterman and B. Kosmin, 'Mapping an unenumerated ethnic population: Jews in London', *Ethnic and Racial Studies*, 9 (1986), 484–501 which elaborates this point, albeit for a late twentieth-century population. See also D. Coleman and J. Salt, 'The ethnic question in the 1991 census: a landmark in British social statistics', in D. Coleman and J. Salt, *Ethnicity in the 1991 census. Volume 1: Demographic characteristics of the ethnic minority population* (London, [1996]), 1–32.

54 This method is recommended in Waterman and Kosmin, 'Mapping an unenumerated ethnic population'. See also the analysis in Jacobs, *Jewish statistics*, 33–5.

55 For example, prior to 1882 the East End received Jewish immigrants from Germany and the Netherlands.

56 In essence, if a household was identified as containing an individual born in eastern Europe, all of the household members related to this individual were treated as east European, regardless of place of birth.

57 White, *Rothschild buildings*, 79. However, other national groups expressed the perceived differences between themselves and other Jewish nationalities in different ways.

58 See M. A. Clarke, 'Household and family in Bethnal Green, 1851–71. The effects of social and economic change', unpublished PhD thesis (Cambridge, 1986).

59 Sweating was a term first used by journeymen tailors to describe those who worked at home, aided by family members, especially their wives and daughters. The term was later expanded to embody those who employed others in the home, in addition to their own family. Thus the 'sweater' was a small master who made other 'sweat'. As Charles Booth points out in his survey of occupations in London, the organisation of the 'sweated' trades' took different forms in different occupations. See C. Booth, 'Sweating', in Booth, ed., *Life and labour*, IV (London, 1893), 328–47. See also *House of Lords Select Committee on the Sweating System*, BPP 1890, XVII which reported that there was no such thing as the 'sweating' system *per se* but rather a cycle of long hours and low wages in some trades.

60 However, note that the furniture trade, in particular cabinet making was characterised by aspects of 'sweating'.

61 It should be noted that workers in the chemical industries were excluded from the New Survey of London Life and Labour as they were not considered to be amongst the 'labouring classes'.

62 Unlike the censuses of 1891 to 1911 which were taken at the usual time of late March/early April, the census of 1921 was taken in June. The cause of the delay being the anticipated general strike of that year.

63 *Royal Commission on Alien Immigration*, q.1, 829, q.2, 488. Cited in Feldman, 'The importance of being English', 72.

64 Booth, 'Sweating', 339–40.

65 Potter, 'Jewish community'. See also D. Englander, 'Booth's Jews: the presentation of Jews and Judaism in *Life and Labor of the People in London*', in D. Englander and R. O'Day, eds, *Retrieved riches. Social investigation in Britain, 1840–1914* (Aldershot, [1995]), 289–322.

66 Potter, 'Jewish community', 189.

67 Potter, 'Jewish community', 188.

68 Jacobs, *Jewish statistics*, 25-30. See also Feldman, *Englishmen and Jews*, 149-51.

69 Jacobs, *Jewish statistics*, 22-3.

70 For a broader examination of leaving the parental home in this period see K. Schürer, *Work and leaving home: the experience of England and Wales, 1850–1920*, ESRC Future of Work Programme Working Paper, 12 ([Leeds, 2000]).

71   The categories used in Tables 5 and 6 are based on those described in P. Laslett, 'Introduction: the history of the family', in P. Laslett and R. Wall, eds, *Household and family in past time* (Cambridge, 1972), 1–89. The classification scheme uses as is base the notion of a conjugal family unit (CFU), formed by either married couples, married couples with never-married child(ren) or lone parent families with never-married child(ren). Extended households are those with a single CFU extended by the presence of other resident kin. Multiple households are those with two of more related CFUs present. Households classified as 'Co-resident kin' are those without a CFU, but with two or more co-residing kin, for example, siblings living together without a member of the parental generation present.

72   M. Anderson, *Family structure in nineteenth-century Lancashire* (Cambridge, 1972), 43–56, 164–8.

73   For example, the number of male-headed households to female headed households for the four groups (Bethnal Green born; born within London; born outside of London; east European) were, respectively, 4.5, 4.7, 4.2, and 12.4 in 1911 and 4.1, 4.0, 3.0 and 5.3 in 1921.

74   See, for example, P. Czap, '"A large family: the peasant's greatest wealth": serf households in Mishino, Russia, 1814–1858', in R. Wall, J. Robin and P. Laslett, eds, *Family forms in historic Europe* (Cambridge, 1983), 105–50; M. Mitterauer and A. Kagan, 'Russian and central European Family structures: a comparative view', *Journal of Family History*, 7 (1982), 103–31; A. Plakans, 'Interaction between the household and the kin group in the eastern European past: posing the problem', *Journal of Family History*, 12 (1987), 163–75; and also the comparative tables provided in P. Laslett, 'Family and household as work and kin groups', in R. Wall, , J. Robin and P. Laslett, eds, *Family forms in historic Europe* (Cambridge, 1983), 513–63.

75   The term 'inmate' is used to indicate both boarders and lodgers attached to the main household group.

76   Never-married offspring are children or step-children of the household head who have not yet married. A married child of the household head is counted as a co-resident relative, as is, say a widowed father, living with a son or daughter who is designated as head.

77   Anderson, *Family structure,* 166–8.

78   It should be noted that continental Jews were noted in the nineteenth century for a pattern of early marriage. See Jacobs, *Jewish statistics,* 50-2.

79   For example, many of the Jewish immigrants were eventually settled in newly-built tenement model dwellings. See White, *Rothschild buildings.*

Contributors

Jim Galloway is a researcher at the Centre for Metropolitan History, part of the University of London's Institute of Historical Research. He has published extensively on town-country relations in the late medieval and early modern periods, focusing especially upon London's dynamic role within the economy of its region and of England as a whole.

Craig Spence is a lecturer in historical studies in the Department of Historical and Cultural Studies, Goldsmiths' College, University of London. He has research interests in early modern culture and society, especially in relation to London.

Graham Mooney is a post-doctoral research fellow at the Wellcome Trust Centre for the History of Medicine at UCL. He is working on a project assessing the impact of infectious disease notification on the practice of medicine in modern Britain. He is interested in the histories of British public health and demography and interactions between the two.

Kevin Schürer is Director of the UK Data Archive and Research Professor in History at the University of Essex. His current research interests focus on the interaction of work and family in the nineteenth and early twentieth centuries; the examination of patterns of isonomy and regional identities; and the comparative analysis of historical census data.